George Orwell

Volume Seven
No. 1

George Orwell

Publishing Office
Abramis Academic
ASK House
Northgate Avenue
Bury St. Edmunds
Suffolk
IP32 6BB
UK

Tel: +44 (0)1284 717884
Fax: +44 (0)1284 717889
Email: info@abramis.co.uk
Web: www.abramis.co.uk

Copyright
All rights reserved. No part of this publication may be reproduced in any material form (including photocopying or storing it in any medium by electronic means, and whether or not transiently or incidentally to some other use of this publication) without the written permission of the copyright owner, except in accordance with the provisions of the Copyright, Designs and Patents Act 1988, or under terms of a licence issued by the Copyright Licensing Agency Ltd, 33-34, Alfred Place, London WC1E 7DP, UK. Applications for the copyright owner's permission to reproduce part of this publication should be addressed to the Publishers.

© 2022 George Orwell Studies & Abramis Academic

ISSN 2399-1267
ISBN 978-1-84549-808-5

George Orwell

Contents

Editorial
The Special Art of Editing and Annotating – by Richard Lance Keeble — Page 3

Papers
'A Great Prop of the School': The Important Place of Sunderland Church High School in Understanding Eileen O'Shaughnessy – by Angela Smith — Page 6

Seeing What is In Front of One's Nose: George Orwell's Representation of Social Reality – by Dominic Angeloch — Page 23

Articles
The Elephant in the Room: Reassessing the Genre of George Orwell's 'Shooting an Elephant' – by Carol Biederstadt — Page 41

Retracing Orwell's Steps in Wigan – Balancing Curiosity with Respect – by Timothy Foster — Page 47

Authors and Titles Mentioned in *The Road to Wigan Pier* – by L. J. Hurst — Page 50

Reflections on 'St Andrew's Day, 1935' – by Douglas Kerr — Page 53

Why He Joined the I. L. P: Orwell, Brockway and the Struggle for Socialism – by John Newsinger — Page 61

Mary Poppins at the Ministry of Tweets – by John Rodden — Page 80

Orwell's Rats – by Darcy Moore — Page 92

Book reviews
Darcy Moore on *Orwell and Empire*, by Douglas Kerr; Richard Lance Keeble on *Complete Drama Reviews by George Orwell*, edited by Cole Davis, *Complete Book Reviews by George Orwell*, edited by Cole Davis and *Revenge is Sour: Lesser-Known Short Works by George Orwell*, edited by Cole Davis; Dennis Glover on *Becoming George Orwell: Life and Letters, Legend and Legacy*, by John Rodden — Page 102

Editors
Richard Lance Keeble — University of Lincoln
Tim Crook — Goldsmiths, University of London

Reviews Editor
Megan Faragher — Wright State University

Production Editor
Paul Anderson — University of Essex

Editorial Board
Kristin Bluemel — Monmouth University, New Jersey
Dorian Lynskey — Author, journalist
Peter Marks — University of Sydney
John Newsinger — Bath Spa University
Marina Remy — Paris Sorbonne
John Rodden — University of Texas at Austin
Jean Seaton — University of Westminster
Peter Stansky — Stanford University, US
D. J. Taylor — Author, journalist, biographer of Orwell
Martin Tyrrell — Queen's University, Belfast
Nathan Waddell — University of Birmingham
Florian Zollmann — Newcastle University

With editorial assistance from Marja Giejgo

EDITORIAL

The Special Art of Editing and Annotating

Peter Davison, who passed away on 16 August 2022, was a giant amongst Orwellian scholars. His editing of the 20-volume *Complete Works* amounts, as D. J. Taylor comments, 'to one of the triumphs of late 20th century publishing'. *George Orwell Studies* is to pay special tribute to Professor Davison in its next issue.

Since the lifting of copyright restrictions on Orwell's works in 2020, 70 years after his death, a number of publishers have brought out re-issues – but none can hope to match Davison's masterly editing and the dazzling depth and range of his annotations.

Cole Davis, of the Norwich-based Volitor publishers, is to be commended for bringing out all of Orwell's book reviews in one massive tome, thus providing an invaluable resource for researchers and literary critics (see my review on page 107). But the introductory comments and annotations bear no comparison to Davison's.

On the other hand, Nathan Waddell, of Birmingham University, has made a tremendous contribution to our understanding of one of Orwell's most neglected novels with his editing and annotating of *A Clergyman's Daughter* (Oxford University Press, 2021). Orwell himself was his sternest critic, describing the novel in a letter to novelist Henry Miller as 'bollox' and, significantly, he did not allow it to be reprinted or translated during his lifetime.

In this context, Waddell has performed a remarkable feat, arguing persuasively, both through his Introduction and in the meticulous and always interesting annotations, that the novel has many fascinating (and too often missed) literary aspects but also offers many unique insights into how Orwell became the internationally celebrated author of *Animal Farm* (1945) and *Nineteen Eighty-Four* (1949). In addition to the 224 'Explanatory Notes' at the end, the Introduction is accompanied by 60 footnotes, all of this reflecting the vast research involved. Waddell's writing is, as Orwell would have approved, always clear, engaging and free from highfalutin, abstract theorising.

As Orwell's works are republished, editors have a responsibility to offer new insights in their introductions and annotations. Waddell

RICHARD LANCE KEEBLE

certainly meets this requirement with aplomb. *A Clergyman's Daughter* is generally seen as apolitical and in no way as 'engaged' as the novels either side of it – *Burmese Days* (1934) and *Keep the Aspidistra Flying* (1936) – and certainly not as politically sensitive as the later *Coming Up for Air* (1939), *Animal Farm* and *Nineteen Eighty-Four*. Here Waddell highlights a preoccupation with the problem of class and the injustices of wealth. Although the 'horrible communism' of the Trafalgar Square down-and-outs is not of the Bolshevik variety, their plight captures what Dorothy understands as 'the mysterious power of money' (p. xxiii).

At the novel's literal and symbolic midpoint there's an extended depiction of the 'horrible futility' of destitution as Orwell draws an implicit contrast between the bony frames of the beggars and the 'class instinct' of those who, like Sir Thomas, seemingly care so little about 'visions of poverty and of escape from poverty' (ibid). Waddell adds: 'The novel's gentle mockery of "electioneering", an attitude established principally through its sardonic representations of Mr Blifil-Gordon's by-election campaign, anticipates similar material in *Coming Up for Air*, but it also arguably reveals how difficult it can be to incorporate political themes into domestic stories in a convincing way' (ibid). Yet, the novel is attentive to the ways in which individuals reproduce large-scale political dynamics in the smaller spaces of home and work. Waddell sums up – elegantly – the novel's engagement with politics as both important and 'oblique': a 'matter of peeking round corners and of subtle evocations' (p. xxiv).

The disjointed structure of *A Clergyman's Daughter* – with Dorothy Hare moving from the dull confines of her vicarage home in Knype Hill, to Trafalgar Square with its down-and-outs, to the hopfields of south-east London, to Mrs Creevy's appalling Ringwood House Academy before returning to her home town and her old life – has often drawn the wrath of critics. Orwell is clearly putting his own experiences to use in the novel. Yet, Waddell argues that this very lack of integration 'might, in fact, be precisely the book's point: its attempt to embody, at the levels of generic shifts and episodic transitions, Dorothy's struggle to find rest in a changing world' (p. xiii).

Waddell's annotations add still more to the enjoyment and understanding of the novel. Authors (both famous and obscure) cited include Hans Christian Andersen, Baudelaire, Boccaccio, Bunyan, Lewis Carroll, Warwick Deeping, Dickens, Eliot, Freud, Galsworthy, Gibbon, Goldsmith, Anna Maria Hall, Felicia Hemans, Horace, Thomas Hughes, Julian Huxley, Keats, John Maynard Keynes, John Kensit, D. H. Lawrence, Longfellow, Petronius, Bertrand Russell, Shakespeare (many times), Swift, Trollope, Tennyson, John and Charles Wesley and Wordsworth – all this reflecting the wide reading of both Orwell and Waddell. A range of newspapers are also cited including the *Daily Mail*, *Daily Telegraph*, *Church Times*, *News Chronicle*, *High Churchman's Gazette*, *Sporting Times* and the invented *Pippin's Weekly* and *Sunday Spyhole*. And I counted 25 religious (*Bible*, *Book of Common Prayer* etc) references.

Waddell is also keen to stress the *pleasure* he derives from reading the novel. He writes of the enjoyment to be had 'from the countryside sequence' and Orwell's detailing 'the technicalities of hop picking and from his evocative descriptions of the smell and feel of getting in among leaves and branches' (p. xviii). Similarly, much of the pleasure from reading about Dorothy's ordeal at Ringwood House 'comes from the fact that he barely veils his disgust at its educational standards' (ibid).

Waddell's editing, in fact, amounts to an outstanding scholarly achievement – very much in the tradition of Peter Davison.

Richard Lance Keeble,
University of Lincoln

PAPER

'A Great Prop of the School': The Important Place of Sunderland Church High School in Understanding Eileen O'Shaughnessy

ANGELA SMITH

This paper explores the relevance of Sunderland Church High School for Girls in understanding the life and beliefs of Eileen O'Shaughnessy, George Orwell's first wife. It will take account of education reforms, and look at how the influential head teacher, Miss Ironside, instigated changes in the school that benefited Eileen and led to her studying at Oxford University before working in London. The love of education that Ironside instilled returned to Eileen in the early 1930s and contributed to her enrolling on an MA which in turn led to her meeting Eric Blair. The skills and resourcefulness that she started to develop at Sunderland Church High set her in good stead to survive as a single woman in the 1930s. Drawing on archive material, the paper shows how Eileen embraced school life and how her teachers perceived and encouraged Eileen in her formative years.

Key words: Eileen O'Shaughnessy, educational reform, gender and education, single women, First World War

Eileen Maud O'Shaughnessy was born in South Shields, in the north-east of England, on 25 September 1905. While her Irish-born parents had moved around the United Kingdom through her father's job, South Shields was to be the first location where they would settle for any length of time; the Tyneside town providing a stable place to bring up their two children. From here, Eileen's life may have followed the path of similarly well brought-up middle class young ladies to marriage and motherhood had it not been for two things: the First World War and Eileen's burning ambition to do as well as, if not better than, her elder brother, Laurence. Sylvia Topp's excellent biography of Eileen (2020) dwells upon the disappointment Eileen felt at the conclusion of her university studies, where the academic post her abilities warranted was denied by a dominant culture of misogyny. However, this led to Eileen taking up work in London, before then re-entering academic study ten years after graduating. It was through this return to study that she encountered Eric Blair, the man she was to marry. Eileen and Eric met at a party hosted by a mutual friend and married within a year. Out of the thwarted dreams of her early career, Eileen entered a life where she came to have a huge influence on some of the most famous English literary works in the 20th century.

But what influences pervaded the early part of Eileen's journey from South Shields to London, by way of Oxford? This has been a difficult question to answer since the school Eileen attended from 1915-1924, Sunderland Church High School for Girls, closed in 2017 with its records scattered or destroyed. However, enough can be retrieved to give us a picture of just what was so attractive about the school that inspired Eileen to undertake the hour-long journey by train and tram every day to attend.

This paper, therefore, looks at the school in the context of Eileen's time and explores how the influence of the head teacher helped form the ambitious, out-going, confident young lady who went to Oxford.

GENDER AND EDUCATION

Britain only made education compulsory and free for the under-12s in 1870 when the Education Act was finally passed after many years of debate in parliament. The Act provided free education for boys and girls. Before this, education had been provided on an *ad hoc* basis, often guided by long-standing assumptions that girls would find no benefit in education beyond basic literacy, numeracy and practical household management. Indeed, young women were considered to lack femininity if they exhibited intelligence beyond their domestic remit, a stereotype that had a long history and was central to the patriarchal ideology of the time. We still have the legacy of this bias against learned women built into our Higher Education system, where an undergraduate degree is styled a Bachelor's degree, with the next tier of qualification called a Master's. Before the 1870 Act, there was virtually no opportunity for women to enter the higher level of education in the UK, as only a tiny number of British universities would countenance their admission (the University of London was the first to admit women in 1869 (Carter 2018)). Whilst the Act placed no restraint on boys and girls being educated together, most fee-paying schools continued to teach genders separately, thereby reproducing the stereotypes of boys being educated to go into the world of work that included business, science and the military, while training girls to run a household (either their own or someone else's). The division of what were considered to be appropriate subjects by gender was largely unchanged across the social classes, perhaps with greater opportunities for resources being the only advantage enjoyed by girls from wealthier homes.

Sunderland Church High School, at this time, was following the pattern of traditional gender stereotypes. One of four independent (that is to say, not state-funded) schools in the area, it was run by the Church of England under the management of a board of trustees attached to the Church Schools Company. These catered for the new middle class that emerged during the 19th century, able to pay for educational advantage. Other Church high schools opened in 1884 and 1885: those in Newcastle and Gateshead were close to South Shields, with a third further afield in Durham. As was usual in such schools, girls and boys were educated separately, to different curricula. However, this reinforced gender division, with the middle-class girls being educated in 'accomplishments' such as needlework, music, painting and dancing, with additional focus on skills that would allow them to manage a household and children. In contrast, boys' education mirrored the Classics taught in the longer-established and upper-class private school system, with additional subjects in the sciences and engineering that catered for the emerging middle-class occupations. To give this gender division context, it is estimated that only one in fifty middle-class women entered paid employment on leaving school (Holden 2007).

By the beginning of the 20th century, attitudes were starting to change, partly mirroring the rise in arguments for women's rights in the century's first decades, typified by the disparate movements demanding women's right to the vote (Stevens 2007). Sunderland Church High School was not immune from these challenges to gender roles, particularly under the influence of the head teacher, Miss Ethel Ironside. In the next section, we will suggest that Ironside's reputation as a moderniser, pursuing a more progressive approach to teaching and learning, may well have been a factor in Mr and Mrs O'Shaughnessy's decision to send Eileen to that school rather than any of the others that were in easier reach.

THE NEW WOMAN AS HEAD TEACHER

Ironside attended Cheltenham Ladies' College, where the renowned Miss Dorothea Beale (1831-1906) had already educated young women in a range of subjects that would be comparable with the studies of young men (Kamm 1958). Such young women were the first to go to university, aided by many of the 'new' universities such as Manchester and Newcastle which were willing to offer degrees to women. Revealing a deep cultural misogyny, the most esteemed and ancient universities, Oxford and Cambridge, were still some years away from allowing female students to graduate (Oxford was the first to offer degrees to women in 1920, whilst Cambridge held back until 1948). Ironside took a teaching qualification at London University and began a career that would eventually lead her to Sunderland.

When Ironside arrived at Sunderland Church High School in 1905, the school was in a crisis with only 53 pupils registered. This was partly explained by local competition in the opening of a Higher Grade School (the forerunner of the later secondary schools) in Sunderland in 1890, charging a nominal fee of just tuppence (2d) a week. While fees at Church High varied according to factors such as the additional classes the girls attended and whether they had a sister already in the school, fees were markedly above those required for the Higher Grade School.

Ironside could be described as a 'new woman' of this period. The term 'new woman' derives from Henry James and his irreverent modern heroines Daisy Miller (in novel of the same name, in 1879) and Isabel Archer (in *Portrait of a Lady*, of 1881). Betsy Israel explains:

> Unlike the average bohemian or bachelor girl, the new woman possessed a leftist intellectual pedigree. Her attitudes and beliefs were descended from the elite early feminists [and in the United States] the single blessed spinsters of the [US] Civil War era and later reformers who'd helped found or been among the first to attend the women's colleges (2002: 114).

Ironside regularly took part in sports activities with the girls (including swimming and hockey), as well as teaching sciences and mathematics. She was also familiar with 'modern' teaching techniques, advocating the Froebel kindergarten methods at the school. This method allowed children to grow and develop at their own pace, nurtured by knowledgeable and supportive educators, thus placing less emphasis on traditional learning by rote methods (Brosterman 1997). In 1911, Ironside was obliged to defend this system of education to parents whose chief concerns were the delivery of rapid results. At that time she commented: 'Those who trust their children to the care of the kindergarten must be content to await patiently the results which must ultimately show themselves in quickness of observations and intelligent grasp of subjects' (in Sayers 1984: 27). In terms of her overall project, Ironside was setting up the school to have a steady progression of girls from Kindergarten up to Senior and encouraging parents to 'stick with the system' for the duration.

ANGELA SMITH

Miss Ethel Ironside in the 1930s, reproduced courtesy of Audrey M. Sayers

At her first prize-giving event in 1908, Ironside set out what would become her philosophy on educating the young women in her charge:

> Our highest hope is to send out into the world a race of women of sane balanced mind, able to take a keen and intelligent interest in all that is going forward, proud of their nation because not ignorant of its great history, wide minded and not insular because they know something of languages and peoples other than their own, imperially minded because they have been taught of the responsibilities and duties of a citizen of such an Empire as that of Great Britain, eager to read and form judgements for themselves, able to appreciate beauty with both eye and ear, able to reason, able to listen; in short, women with training, and not ignorant, gossiping idle beings, whose chief fault, nay, misfortune, is in being the possessors of ill-stocked minds. What are going to be the problems with which this generation of girls will have to grapple in their turn is not the point; the thing is that they shall be taught to use wisdom along whatever path they may be sent – and wisdom the beginning of which is fear of the Lord (quoted in Sayers 1984: 28).

If we look at the details of what Ironside is promoting in this address, we will see the school represented as a collective endeavour under her leadership, geared to confront the damaging stereotypes associated with women. The stereotypical qualities accorded to women are expressed baldly, as 'ignorant, gossiping idle beings'. In patriarchal society, men are associated with rational thought and temperance, with women assumed to be deficient in such attributes.

Ironside presents an opposing view: that the girls at Sunderland Church High School will be 'of sane balanced mind' and will not conform to any disobliging female stereotype. The underlying assumption is a Sunderland Church High education equips girls with knowledge of the world that would be useful beyond the home. Ironside's framing of the alternative as a 'misfortune', with the deliberate correction from 'chief fault', propels her stated commitment that it is through education that women can do good in this world, rather than being confined to the home. The girls will also be engaged with the outside world, in arriving at a considered and informed view of matters of shared concern and public importance. This refutes the stereotype of female domesticity, where the concerns of the woman are associated with the private sphere whilst those of men are associated with the 'public sphere'.

In terms of addressing these public concerns, the mention of Empire has considerable contemporary resonance. It would have been just five years since the end of the Boer Wars, a time when the British army had not won the quick, decisive victory predicted. It is also preparing the young women of the school to take an active role in the maintenance of imperial power.

IDENTITY AND ETHOS IN THE SCHOOL

In 1907, one of Ironside's first initiatives was to introduce a school uniform that comprised box-pleated gym tunics, white blouses and ties. This helped to create a sense of unity amongst the girls and to ameliorate the snobbery that Ironside had observed amongst some of the girls who regarded their clothing as indicating social class. The uniform initiated by Ironside continued to adapt to fashion and cultural acceptability: the only known photograph of Eileen at school shows her wearing the version of this uniform adopted after 1907, with the slightly shorter skirt and no tie.

A still more tangible instance of Ironside's commitment to an ethos of equality and virtue was the link she made between the school and the local Royal Infirmary. There, the girls were engaged in charitable work such as sewing garments to distribute in the children's ward and raising funds through 'entertainments' which included staging plays, concerts and hosting tea parties. These activities met with such success that they were quickly adopted by the other Church High Schools in the region. The school

Eileen (left) with a friend, courtesy of the Orwell Collection, UCL

also formed teams in netball, tennis, swimming and hockey, playing in regional tournaments against teams from other high schools.

Of course, many of these activities, including sewing and holding tea parties, remain within conventional gender boundaries. Furthermore, traditional subjects were still on the curriculum. Needlework, singing and painting, for example, were all still taught, although there was less emphasis on these subjects. However, the girls were organised in teams and entered local competitions in singing and music. For example, the North of England Music tournament in 1922 awarded the school's Senior Girls' Choir second place, a choir that included Eileen O'Shaughnessy (although her first name appears as 'Elsie' in the school magazine, *The Chronicle,* for this). It is fair to say that the pupils' identification with their gender is encouraged, including an understanding of the expectations and conventions this involves. However, the articulation of this awareness with advocacy and action remains apparent. For example, in 1909, Ironside introduced the debating society, for whom the first topic was 'That women should have the vote and be equal with men'. The motion was carried. If we look at the topic of the debate, it is more than just 'Votes for Women': it includes the point that gender equality beyond enfranchisement is also at issue. It was followed soon afterwards by a parade through Sunderland in support of female enfranchisement, with a group of girls from Sunderland Church High taking part wearing placards reading: 'Votes for Women', all supported by Ironside.

A sense of continuity and investment in each girl was further emphasised by the creation of the Old Girls' Guild in 1908, which involved inviting former pupils to engage with the school at various points and in various capacities. The guild grew, with alumni continuing to be members for many years after leaving school, some of them from their new homes in distant lands. It would also come into Eileen's life as we shall see shortly.

These innovations may have appeared alarming to the more conservative parents in the area, but many traditional arts subjects retained their place in the curriculum. Thus outwardly the school could be presented as progressive, confident and industrious whilst maintaining elements of female decorum.

By 1912, numbers had risen to 142, and had risen still further to 230 the following year. New premises were bought for use by the school in the surrounding area of Ashbrooke, including the development of additional boarding accommodation in Clifton Hall.

THE WAR YEARS 1914-1918

Most organisations that included women and girls engaged in domestically-oriented 'war work'. This was primarily in the form of knitting and sewing parties which provided a steady supply for garments. Sunderland Church High School was no different. The girls took foods, sweets and stationery to wounded men in the Royal Infirmary, and 'adopted' six prisoners of war in Germany (sending them letters and parcels on a weekly basis). Senior girls and staff joined the Sunderland branch of the Red Cross' Voluntary Aid Detachment (VAD). Near by Hammerton Hall was commissioned as a hospital for officers whilst the Royal Infirmary became the destination of ordinary service personnel. There, Sayers (1984: 36) describes how senior girls volunteered as VADs and worked as housemaids and cooks, comprising almost the entire staff in these roles. Even though the usual image of the VAD is of the glamourised nurse, it is clear that the middle-class young women of Church High were willing to occupy roles more associated with servants in their own homes.

The school also continued established activities in drama, tea parties and garden parties for wounded soldiers. In 1917, they had 400 guests at one such event. Overall, the school was wholeheartedly engaging with the war on the home front.

It was into the midst of this engagement that Eileen O'Shaughnessy arrived at the school in 1915 when it was about to adopt the Durham School Certificate (1917), the local examination board qualification equivalent to GCSE today. Eileen was one of seven girls in her year to take the Durham School Certificate successfully in 1921. She was clearly embracing the opportunities it gave her as part of her route to university.

1917 also saw the introduction of the house system. This was done, according to the former teachers interviewed by Sayers (1984 37-8), to help foster a greater sense of cooperation and enthusiasm throughout the school, from the Kindergarten up to the Seniors. The decision was taken to have four 'houses', so following the system already well-established in boys' fee-paying schools. The girls at Sunderland Church High were divided up according to where they lived, using quadrants on a map, while the houses were given names taken from the initials of the school motto *Timor Domini Principium Sapientiae* (TDPS): Tiger (red), Drake (green), Panther (purple) and Swift (blue). In her announcement, reported in *The Chronicle*, Ironside (drawing on military tropes) noted that these 'represent suitable animals or birds as emblems, in addition to being the name of four Destroyers' (November 1918), and that the associated house badge be worn on the left side of the tunic 'in the same way as a military ribbon' (ibid). As her home address fell into the northern quadrant of the roughly-divided local map that Ironside used, Eileen found herself in Swift House. In this way, the school continued to modernise at a pace, and Eileen was able to take advantage of this (the school report for 1923 notes she is 'full of loyal interest in the life of the school'). It is also a model of cultural education adopted by the other Church High Schools in the region around this time, but their houses were less imaginatively named: usually simply after colours.

In 1918, when some women had finally been granted the right to vote in Britain, Ironside urged her girls:

> … to use it with knowledge and balance and judgement, forming a definite opinion not grounded on prejudice or superficiality; there must be sincere study of religious, political and social subjects, and all women who have been High School girls ought to be ready to lay things quite clearly before women less well educated than themselves (cited in Sayers 1984: 26).

Again, Ironside is rejecting restrictive gender stereotypes. The girls at Sunderland Church High would be educated to possess knowledge that was beyond the domestic domain and include 'political and social subjects' (along with the expected religious emphasis that goes with any school set up by a Church organisation). Her comments also mark the girls as being apart from the majority of their sex who are 'less well educated' in these areas, thus presenting them as superior in knowledge but not arrogant. Their knowledge is to be put to good use when voting. Although in 1918 only a minority of women could vote, these would have been middle-class, propertied women such as the girls who attended the school could expect to be.

In these ways, Ironside set about modernising the school, both in its organisation (such as the introduction of the house system) and in its curriculum, with the emphasis on 'political and social subjects' beyond the domestic domain. In encouraging debate and engaging with the wider community, the school was outward looking and progressive. This continued into the First World War, with the curriculum expanded to include a route into university entrance through the Durham University Certification examination. Ironside's influence resulted in a large increase in numbers enrolling at a time when state-run schools were encroaching on the independent schools' territories. For example, the boys' Church High School in Sunderland closed around 1910 as parents chose to send their sons to the Higher Grade School, later Bede School, in Sunderland, and similar ones in the Tyneside area.

The fact that Ironside was introducing a broader curriculum for the girls at the time of the First World War shows she is aware of the future necessity for them to earn a living for themselves without being reliant on a husband to support them. The prescience of Ironside's changes can be seen in retrospect to have been very timely. The inter-war years saw young women such as Eileen O'Shaughnessy complete their school education and go on to university with many of them then able to earn their own living as single women.

SINGLE WOMEN IN THE INTER-WAR YEARS

The number of single women reached record figures in the inter-war years as the consequences of the First World War became clear. Until 1918, it was generally assumed that a single woman was either a widow or else had been deemed unfit for marriage (Bell and Yans 2008: 10). The First World War changed this as the first industrialised war brought with it mass carnage among men of marriageable age. This is clear from the census data:

Unmarried 25-25 years		
(by population in hundreds of thousands)		
	1911	1921
Men	1,091	894
Women	1,109	1,158
"Shortfall"	18	264

This huge increase in the imbalance between the number of men and women of conventional marriageable age would have been even more pronounced for middle-class women such as those who attended Sunderland Church High, as the death rates for middle-class men were proportionally higher in the First World War. This has been said to stem from a combination of the cavalier notion of officers 'leading from the front' and, in the war's early years, distinctive differences in the uniforms of officers from those worn by ordinary soldiers, marking them out more clearly for enemy snipers (Winter 1979).

As Holden (2007) comments in relation to these statistics that more than half of the women who were single in 1921 had not married by the time of the 1931 census. Although the percentage of women who were unmarried (including never married and widowed) in 1921 was remarkably high, this was mostly caused by the huge rise in the number of women widowed by the war. By 1931, however, the number of widows had returned to a level comparable with 1911 as most of them had remarried (Smith 2013). Indeed, many young middle-class women became aware of the likelihood of having no male breadwinner. Essex's (1977) oral history of this time records testimony from women from middle-class backgrounds that reveals they were warned by schools and universities about the shortage of men and that they should make career choices with this in mind. This chimes with the changes Ironside made to the curriculum and culture of Sunderland Church High around the time of Eileen O'Shaughnessy. In fact, Ironside's report in the November 1917 *Chronicle* directly addresses this issue as she warns against the lure of short-term war work in banks and offices, and cites government concerns of a looming teacher shortage. She writes of an:

> … urgent necessity of women training for Education, [encouraging in particular] girls who were in doubt as to whether they ought to spend money on Oxford or Cambridge when they could quite well be earning a weekly salary with no training at all. … If she has a special love for small children, she should certainly take the Froebel Course, and if for older children she must begin working as soon as may be for an entrance to one of the Universities, or if possible for a scholarship (*The Chronicle*, November 1917).

Whilst teaching is seen here as the most desirable profession for young women, the need to gain a university education is marked out for special attention because of the financial implications. To help girls to go to university, Ironside instigated a system of scholarship, specifically aimed at girls who would go to Oxford or Cambridge universities. At that time, even though neither university allowed women to graduate, the value perceived of an education offered at these two universities was temptation enough to apply. Such was the esteem, the school allocated a mistress to coach potential entrants: Eileen's coach was Miss Dyer, the mistress who edited *The Chronicle* as well as teaching English and Latin.

The first scholarship of £30 a year was set up in 1918, funded by the Old Girls' Guild and open to any girl who applied to go any university in the UK. The scholarship was not awarded every year, but the school record book shows that Eileen was awarded it in both 1925 and 1926. The Old Girls' Scholarship shows the changes Ironside made in the school in bringing a greater sense of collaboration and responsibility, even after leaving school. The criteria for awarding the scholarship was not financial need (which would have been rather odd, given the fact that it was a fee-paying school and attracted affluent middle-class families), but rather for exceptional promise.

A second scholarship was instituted in 1919: the Everett Scholarship was funded by the Everett family who donated a

£1,000 War Loan to the school as a thanks-giving offering for the safe return of their son (a former Old Boy at the now-closed Boys' School) from the war. The daughter, Dorothy, had been an Old Girl and she continued to manage the scholarship for many years, ensuring it was safely invested and able to keep up with rising costs. To begin with, Oxbridge entrants were eligible for a grant of £20 per year for three years. Like the Old Girls' Scholarship, this was based solely on academic merit.

In setting up financial incentives to apply to university, the school was encouraging its young women to engage with an education that could be of value beyond the home. On the carved wooden prize boards at the school, it is noticeable that only Eileen O'Shaughnessy's name appears on plaques for both the Old Girls' Scholarship and the Everett Scholarship, showing her to be an exceptionally talented student. Significantly, during the 1930s there was a rule change so that an individual could hold only one scholarship at a time – perhaps to avoid a repeat of Eileen's achievement. She was, nevertheless, quite an exceptional pupil. At the point when she left the school, her positions and awards gained were:

- head girl;
- head prefect;
- Swift House captain;
- sub-editor of *The Chronicle*;
- sub-librarian;
- president of the League of Nations branch;
- Whitaker Thompson Memorial Prize-winner.

This latter prize was named after Mr Whitaker Thompson, who had been chairman of the Church Schools Company for many years and had left a small legacy in the form of this prize in his will. The prize was open to entrants from all the Church High Schools in the region, so Eileen's success in winning this particular prize hints at her talents being recognised more widely.

As Swift House captain, too, Eileen showed herself to be a motivational and enthusiastic leader. In *The Chronicle* for November 1923, she welcomed newcomers to Swift House as a place which 'not only realizes but practices the ideal of fellowship and co-operation'. In lamenting the lack of success on the sporting field in the previous year, she summons a phrase that hints at later socialist beliefs: 'Unity is Strength'.

Honours Board for Everett Scholarship

Overall, it seems Eileen's leadership and organisational qualities were recognised throughout the school, not just in Swift House. Her editing of the school magazine links with her future life as editor of Orwell's work. Furthermore, we can see her interest in politics and international affairs with her involvement in the League of Nations branch which she may well have drawn on as a common interest with Orwell when they met.

UNIVERSITY AND BEYOND

Eileen went to St Hugh's College, Oxford, in the autumn of 1924 to study English Literature. This is recorded in Ironside's column in *The Chronicle* in June 1924:

> Eileen O'Shaughnessy has brought great honour to the School with her English Bursary of £20 per annum for three years at S. Hugh's College, Oxford; and Margaret Ellis also with her entrance to S. Hugh's on her History Scholarship paper. We congratulate them most heartily, and their coaches, Miss Dyer and Miss Curran.

The Chronicle from November 1924 continues in the same tone, describing Eileen and two other university-bound former girls as 'real props of the school'. The enthusiastic and outstanding schoolgirl embraced university life, supported in part by the scholarships she had won from her school as well as the Oxford bursary. As Topp's biography of Eileen shows (202: 41-70), she did well at Oxford, but the university was only just starting to allow female students to graduate and residual misogyny meant very few female students graduated with a First. Eileen, herself, fell victim to this, meaning that her initial dream to spend her days immersed in literature, teaching it at Oxford, were not to be realised. Instead, she tried her hand at teaching.

Teaching was by far the most popular profession for single women at that time; indeed, it had been her mother's pre-marriage occupation. By 1931, it was estimated that more than half of the single professional women aged 35-45 in the UK were teachers: that is one in eleven women who were in paid employment (Holden 2007). Until 1944, married women were obliged to resign their teaching posts. Another option for the highly educated young woman was in the civil service, which also had a marriage bar in place until 1946 (or until 1973 for the Foreign Service) (Civilservant.org.uk). Exacerbating the injustice still further, women at this time earned on average 60-80 per cent less than men for doing the same or a comparable job (Holden 2007). This gender disparity continued well into the latter part of the century and it took the efforts of Second Wave feminists in the 1960s to bring about political action for equal pay (Smith 2017). Education could only help so far, in a society still dominated by patriarchal attitudes.

REPRESENTATIONS OF SINGLE WOMEN

Given Eileen's great love of literature, and in order to emphasise the broader context alluded to at the end of the last section, it will be useful to look at how single women were represented in texts (including one by George Orwell) of this time. By and large, these fell into one of three categories:

- marriage as an institution must be strongly reinforced with single women viewed as 'imaginary widows' bereaved by the war;
- single women are a danger to society, with no husband to control them (these are often represented as 'flappers' in popular imagination);
- single women who are sexually repressed and, thus, untrustworthy or otherwise unreliable.

The image of the widow or quietly grieving fiancé occupies the margins of literature at this time. She is represented as the living legacy of the dead of the First World War. Her position of moral purity and sacrifice makes her suitable for work in teaching, where she comes to occupy the pages of school stories of the period, a photograph of a young soldier, framed in black, unobtrusively sitting on her desk.

In contrast, the Bright Young Things of the 1920s are seen to dance away the nights, attempting to blot out the horror of the recent war with parties and cocktails. As Israel (2002) shows, the care-free flapper is a stock character in literature at this time, as well as in Hollywood movies where actors such as Clara Bow and Louise Brooks play care-free, single women who meet and then marry handsome, wealthy men. She is, thus, contained and made 'respectable' by being absorbed into the patriarchal system after enjoying a period of relative freedom and independence.

The final category is one that we find in many books of this period, where the image of the prudish, frigid spinster is presented as being symbolic of an intimate (and, by extension, domestic) rather than economic problem, particularly for middle-class women. This is the category of single woman that Orwell writes about. In *The Clergyman's Daughter* (1935), he refers to the 'abnormality' of the spinster who resists marriage because of some deep-rooted sexual trauma.

Yet, whilst Eileen's general cheerfulness and sense of humour may have seen her regarded as akin to a flapper, it is clear that she acknowledged a deeper desire to comply with patriarchal order. In a letter to a friend, quoted by Topp (2020: 108), Eileen jokes that she will marry the first man to ask her if she is still single at 30.

Eileen never settled on a steady job after leaving Oxford, but built a reputation as an excellent editor as well as contributing occasional pieces of freelance journalism. She registered as an Old Girl at Sunderland Church High when she left the school in 1924. When the school came to celebrate its 50th anniversary in 1934, it used the Old Girls network to solicit contributions to a special edition of the school magazine, *The Chronicle*, that year. There seems to have been no specific request as to the nature of the contribution, as the published magazine is a mixture of personal recollections, school history pieces and a couple of poems. One of these poems is by Eileen: 'A century's end: 1984'. It looks back at the previous half century of the school and then hypothesises about a less certain future 50 years ahead. This poem is now thought to have been influential in Orwell choosing *Nineteen Eighty-Four* as the title to his best-known book (Coniam 1999, Bowker 2003: 382). Thus, the Old Girls Guild from Sunderland Church High not only helped support Eileen during her university years, but may inadvertently have influenced one of the most famous titles in 20th century literature.

Eileen's fateful decision to return to study, taking an MA in Psychology, led to her meeting Eric Blair at a party of a mutual friend. Whilst she never finished her MA, choosing instead to set up home with her husband – and joining him in Spain (where he was fighting in a Republican militia) in 1937, the enquiring mind and lively sense of fun first recognised by her teachers at Sunderland Church High certainly set her in good stead for the life she spent as wife of George Orwell, at which point the conventional biographies pick up.

CONCLUSIONS

On its own, a study of this period of the 20th century at Sunderland Church High School would reveal the role of individual and institutional agency in fostering a generation of inspired women, determined to establish their democratic rights. However, the study also provides an insight into the formative influence on Eileen O'Shaughnessy: her willingness to extend her efforts and the headteacher's creation of a progressive school culture and ethos.

The changes in society that occurred in relation to gender in the first decade of the 20th century made it more acceptable for middle class women to go out to work, but this was still treated as employment until an offer of marriage came up. The education system took longer to change, with gender divisions in subjects showing an emphasis on domesticity for girls and industry and business for boys. Sunderland Church High School was one of the first to offer a valuable education for girls that could open up opportunities for paid employment for them. This was largely done under the guidance of Ethel Ironside, whose arrival in 1905 heralded changes in the school that included its culture and structure as well as curriculum.

Perhaps it is this air of progressiveness that proved enticing for the O'Shaughnessys when they were looking for a school to send their precocious daughter to in 1915. Eileen certainly seems to have thrived at the school, with the opportunities it offered sowing the roots of what we know her life became later. There are the organisational abilities and leadership that she exhibits in managing her and Orwell's life, allowing him to work on his novels, and particularly in rescuing him from Spain (which he writes about in *Homage to Catalonia*, of 1938).

Her editing work on *The Chronicle* was invaluable experience that she continued when at Oxford and then took to a whole new level when she started editing Orwell's work. Her influence on what we regard as being his greatest work can only be understood when, as Topp points out, we see the original manuscripts she typed and annotated. These are all skills she started to develop at Sunderland Church High. Her engagement with politics was embedded in the curriculum, but clearly seen to be active in her role as president of the League of Nations Branch (that being another of the progressive ideas to come from the ever-inventive Ironside). Eileen also benefited from the financial cushion of the two scholarships she was awarded when at Oxford.

The least that can be said is that Eileen was in the right place at the right time. She arrived at Sunderland Church High at the point where Ironside's innovations and developments were at their most inventive and industrious. She was equipped with knowledge and skills to survive as a single woman in the inter-war years, skills and knowledge that allowed her to supplement the household income after her marriage. The Old Girls network, and the sense of comradery that Ironside fostered in the school inspired Eileen to write a poem that could be said to have influenced one of the greatest novels in English in the 20th century.

REFERENCES

Bell, Rudolph and Yans, Virginia (2008) (eds) *Women on their Own: Interdisciplinary Perspectives on Being Single,* New Brunswick: Rutgers University Press

Bowker, Gordon (2003) *George Orwell,* London: Abacus

Brosterman, Norman (1997) *Inventing Kindergarten,* New York: Harry N Abrams, Inc

ANGELA SMITH

Carter, Philip (2018). The first women at university: Remembering 'the London Nine'. *Times Higher Education*, January 28 https://www.timeshighereducation.com/blog/first-women-university-remembering-london-nine, accessed on 25 August 2022

Civilservant.org.uk (n.d.) Women in the civil service: A history. Available online at https://www.civilservant.org.uk/women-history.html, accessed on 27 July 2022

Coniam, Sally (1999) Orwell and the origins of *Nineteen Eighty-Four*, *Times Literary Supplement*, 31 December

Essex, Rosamund (1977) *Woman in a Man's World*, London: Sheldon Press

Holden, Katherine (2007) *The Shadow of Marriage: Singleness in England 1914-60*, Manchester: Manchester University Press

Israel, Betsy (2002) *Bachelor Girl: The Secret History of Single Women in the Twentieth Century*, New York: William Morrow

Kamm, Josephine (1958) *How Different From Us: A Biography of Miss Buss and Miss Beale*, London: The Bodley Head

Sayers, Audrey B. (1984) *Sunderland Church High School for Girls: A Centenary History*, Privately printed

Smith, Angela (2013) *Discourses Surrounding British Widows of the First World War*, London: Bloomsbury

Smith, Angela (2017) Introduction *Re-Reading Spare Rib*, Basingstoke: Palgrave

Stevens, Anne (2007) *Women, Power and Politics*, Basingstoke: Palgrave

Topp, Sylvia (2020) *Eileen: The Making of George Orwell*, London: Unbound

Winter, Denis (1979) *Death's Men: Soldiers of the Great War*, London: Penguin

PRIMARY SOURCES

The Chronicle (school magazine for Sunderland Church High School): November 1917, November 1918, June 1922, November 1923, June 1924, November 1924, June 1934

Additional primary sources from Sunderland Church High's archive held at Sunderland Antiquarian Society are reproduced with the consent of that organisation.

NOTE ON THE CONTRIBUTOR

Angela Smith is Professor of Language and Culture at the University of Sunderland, UK. She has published extensively in the areas of gender, media discourse and politeness theory, and edits the Bloomsbury Library of Gender in Popular Culture. She co-runs the Rebel Women of Sunderland project with Sunderland Culture.

PAPER

Seeing What is In Front of One's Nose: George Orwell's Representation of Social Reality

DOMINIC ANGELOCH

George Orwell's prose may appear simple and plain but this is the result of a highly complex style that is 'multi-perspectively' designed and systematically oriented towards achieving insight and understanding – it employs multiple narrative techniques and artful narrative strategies to hold the reader's attention. The central object of Orwell's writing is to convey the complexities of experience. Orwell's prose makes the acquisition of experience itself conscious by constantly opening up insight into the determining conditions of experience in the real world as well as in aesthetic experience. Firstly, the paper casts a spotlight on some of the preconditions for the development of Orwell's writing as they presented themselves in the period after his return to England from Burma. Against this background, it will trace how Orwell's style, his characteristic way of representing reality, especially in its social dimensions, unfolds in Down and Out in Paris and London. *A detailed analysis will then show why and in what ways we see Orwell's style developed to mastery in* The Road to Wigan Pier.

'To see what is in front of one's nose needs a constant struggle.'
(George Orwell, 1946)

With *Animal Farm* and *Nineteen Eighty-Four*, George Orwell became one of the world's most important and influential authors of the 20th century. Before that, from 1922-1927, he was a police officer in Burma witnessing the consequences of Britain's colonial rule. During the early 1930s he experienced poverty and homelessness in France and England; fought as a Republican volunteer against Franco's fascists in the Spanish Civil War in 1937; from 1941-1943, he worked as a talks producer for the BBC's Eastern Service while in 1945 he reported on the end of the Second World War in Germany and France as a correspondent for the *Observer*.[1]

His way of reflecting and representing social and historical reality, which he encountered in the process, is still as unique as it is unrivalled. It is not an exaggeration to say that Orwell created a

DOMINIC ANGELOCH

completely new form of literature. It takes its starting point in his own experience. In 1937, while fighting in a Republican militia in the Spanish Civil War, he wrote to his publisher during a short leave in Barcelona: 'It is not easy here to get hold of any facts outside the circle of one's own experience, but with that limitation I have seen a great deal that is of immense interest to me. ... I hope I shall get a chance to write the truth about what I have seen' (Orwell 2010: 78). Indeed, the search for a true expression for what he has seen and experienced guides Orwell's works throughout his career as an author and journalist.

> Orwell does possess a powerful mind, and his clear-seeming style in his essays is the result of deliberate craftsmanship; he is the practitioner of an artful set of techniques, a complicated strategy for engaging the minds of readers. In all of his essays, especially those in the 1940s, Orwell is examining and clarifying what he thinks, what everyone thinks, and what the reader thinks now but ought to be thinking instead. He is creating the means through which we can learn to think about how our minds operate (Cain 2007: 80).

Orwell's style seems 'invisible' because it does not display itself overtly as a style, as the literary business, obsessed with marketable uniqueness, has demanded both in Orwell's time as well as to this day, and has accordingly also shaped forms of reading and perception.

The form and content of Orwell's texts are highly complex, 'multi-perspectively' designed and systematically oriented towards achieving insight and understanding. The starting point and basis, both the means and central object of his writing and what it brings about in the reader, is experience. 'Aesthetic experience,' writes literary theorist Wolfgang Iser, 'makes the acquisition of experience itself conscious; the emergence of experience is accompanied by the constant insight into the determining conditions' (Iser 1994 [1976]: 217, author's translation). This is precisely what Orwell's work does like no other: his novels, stories and essays present the results of perception, experience and cognition clearly and sharply, unfold a critique of perception (and the ideology contained in it) as well as the world *and*, at the same time, provide us with the means to bring about this critique ourselves. They enable us to see ourselves in that in which we are (cf. ibid: 218).

Following his return from Burma to England in 1927, Orwell's practical, political and literary programme was to broaden his own perspectives and to immerse himself systematically in foreign worlds of experience: 'I wanted to submerge myself, to get right down among the oppressed, to be one of them and on their side against their tyrants,' he writes in retrospect of this time in *The Road to Wigan Pier*, published in 1937 (Orwell 2010 [1937]: 138). Looking back, he describes this programme as a search for the repressed, invisible parts of reality or, more precisely, of social reality – a journey to the very bottom, to what is 'down below', i.e. the bottom of the social 'underworld'. One of the main impulses for embarking on this journey was Orwell's hope to assuage the guilt he felt for having worked for the 'racket' of imperialism in Burma:

> What I profoundly wanted, at that time, was to find some way of getting out of the respectable world altogether. ... I could go among these people, see what their lives were like and feel myself temporarily part of their world. Once I had been among them and accepted by them, I should have touched bottom, and – this is what I felt: I was aware even then that it was irrational – part of my guilt would drop from me (ibid: 140).

According to Jacobson, 'The ex-policeman, ex-public schoolboy, could disprove the harshest judgments he had made against himself, and believed others to have made, only by voluntarily taking it on himself to serve out the harshest sentence society could impose upon those it rejected and condemned' (Jacobson 1971: 50). Indeed, Orwell was determined to reverse as far as possible the upbringing and education in the class-specific prejudices at the boarding schools of the British elite, which he was later to portray, along with their methods, so vividly in his (part fictional, part factual) memoir 'Such, such were the joys', written while working on *Nineteen Eighty-Four*. The aim: to see reality, especially in its social dimensions, as it really is. In his experiences in Burma and the guilt he felt he had brought upon himself during his time there, Orwell identifies the essential impetus for broadening his perspective and turning his interest to what was happening in his own country, his own immediate environment, right before his eyes. Through his observations of those oppressed by the British imperial colonial system and his identification with them, which ran directly counter to his profession and his position in the social hierarchy, his attention now focuses on the victims of the injustice, oppression and exploitation for which he felt he was partly responsible: the workers and the unemployed, the vagrants, the homeless, beggars and petty criminals in Britain – the pariahs on his – and our – own doorstep:

> It was in this way that my thoughts turned towards the English working class. It was the first time that I had ever been really aware of the working class, and to begin with it was only because they supplied an analogy. They were the symbolic

DOMINIC ANGELOCH

victims of injustice, playing the same part in England as the Burmese played in Burma. In Burma the issue had been quite simple. The whites were up and the blacks were down, and therefore as a matter of course one's sympathy was with the blacks. I now realised that there was no need to find tyranny and exploitation. Here in England, down under one's feet, were the submerged working class, suffering miseries which in their different way were as bad as any an oriental ever knows (Orwell 2014 [1937]: 138).

'But,' Orwell continues, 'I knew nothing about working-class conditions … all this was outside the range of my experience' (ibid: 139). And how can one write about something one knows nothing about, even if it is happening right outside your own front door?

I now want to trace how Orwell worked out the possibility of narrating this concrete reality via the experience of it drawing on the theories of Walter Benjamin, who, in his 'Storyteller' essay (1968 [1936]: 84), argued that narrating is essentially 'the ability to exchange experiences'. I will show this by first explaining some of the preconditions for the development of Orwell's writing as they presented themselves in the period after his return to England from Burma. Against this background, I will trace how Orwell's style, his characteristic way of representing reality, especially in its social dimensions, unfolds in *Down and Out in Paris and London*. Finally, I will show in a detailed analysis that, why, and in what ways we see Orwell's style developed to mastery in *The Road to Wigan Pier*.

THE METHOD OF IMMERSION: THE JACK LONDON MODEL

Orwell's exploration of the lives of workers and the poor has several precursors and models in both literature and academia, including Charles Dickens and George Gissing, whom Orwell admired, or works such as the two-volume *The Life and Labour of the People of London* (1902–1903) by the social reformer Charles Booth, which Orwell had already read as a student at Eton.[2] But the direct model for Orwell's method of immersion was Jack London.[3] Orwell had already read *The People of the Abyss* (1903), his account of living with the impoverished and down-and-outs in the East End of London, while at Eton, and even in 1946, he referred to London's book as 'sociologically valuable' (Orwell 1968 [1945a]: 25; see also: Beadle 1978: 190). In the 'Author's Preface', London writes:

> The experiences related in this volume fell to me in the summer of 1902. I went down into the under-world of London with an attitude of mind which I may best liken to that of the explorer. I was open to be convinced by the evidence of my eyes, rather than by the teachings of those who had not seen, or by the

words of those who had seen and gone before. Further, I took with me certain simple criteria with which to measure the life of the under-world. That which made for more life, for physical and spiritual health, was good; that which made for less life, which hurt, and dwarfed, and distorted life, was bad (1982 [1903]: 5).

The three central terms in this passage are 'experiences', 'explorer' and 'evidence of my own eyes'. London introduces himself to his readers as an explorer who undertakes an expedition into the abyss of London's social 'underworld' in order to get an authentic picture of the conditions there with his own eyes. Here, too, the principle of all observation is: real life can only be described on the condition that one has experienced and lived it oneself.

The first chapter of *The People of the Abyss* is entitled 'The descent' and, as with the descent into the underworld of ancient Hades, it opens with a series of warnings intended to dissuade the first-person narrator, London, from his intention to see things for himself. London responds: 'What I wish to do is to go down into the East End and see things for myself. I wish to know how those people are living there, and why they are living there, and what they are living for. In short, I am going to live there myself' (ibid).

For London, immersing one's own body into that which is to be explored and then narrated is the essential prerequisite for the authentic truth of the narrative. One's own view determines the path of research as well as its results: what has not been experienced first-hand cannot be the subject of examination.

'WRITE THE TRUTH ABOUT WHAT I HAVE SEEN': DESCRIBING REALITY – WRITING FROM EXPERIENCE

London's *The People of the Abyss* was a 'clear source of inspiration' for Orwell (Shelden 1991: 132); he followed London's example, sometimes down to the details. When Orwell began his expeditions into the East End in the autumn of 1927, which would then take him into France over the next five years, he, like London, buys old clothes in a pawnshop in order to avoid looking out of place, initially walks the same streets as London, and, like him, tries to suppress his accent, which would make him identifiable as a member of the upper classes. London's *The People of the Abyss* provided Orwell with possibilities for a methodical approach to investigating the social 'underworld' and was at the same time a model for a literary form capable of representing what he had experienced.

But in method as well as in matters of literary form, Orwell quickly broke away from this model. While Jack London rented a pleasant flat nearby for his trips to the East End – 'to assure myself that good clothes and cleanliness still existed' (London 1982 [1903]:

DOMINIC ANGELOCH

19) –, Orwell sleeps in 'spikes' and rented rooms with working-class families while examining the plight of the miners and unemployed in northern England.

This already indicates one of the essential differences between Orwell and his role model: even if London's agenda was to expose himself to the situations he wanted to describe – London never went as far as Orwell. And that is the difference: 'London observes; Orwell participates' (Perkins 1992: 13).

In the years from 1927 to 1936, Orwell dedicated himself to getting to know the conditions of life of the 'invisible' people on the lower edges of society, the workers and casual labourers, the unemployed and beggars, by experiencing and living through them first-hand. 'Orwell's corrective to such falsity,' writes Margery Sabin, 'comes first by immersion of his own body – a supreme measure of truth for Orwell – directly into the experience of misery' (Sabin 2007: 45).

This programmatic immersion of *the author's body in what is to be narrated* is then, also, an essential condition for the possibility of *the reader's immersion in what is narrated*. Reality for the reader is not only what the text manifestly tells, what it gives to think about or what it may aim at in its agenda. What is decisive is above all what the reader can *experience* from the text. Just like his predecessor London, Orwell trusts that what has been observed and experienced in reality can be experienced by the reader as authentic and real through the mediation of the text.

'AT PRESENT I DO NOT FEEL THAT I HAVE SEEN MORE THAN THE FRINGE OF POVERTY'

Orwell's first investigative work took him, following Jack London's example, to London's East End in 1927, then to France and later to the north of England, where he researched the plight of the miners and unemployed. Over a period of five years, Orwell repeatedly lived for long periods as a tramp, slept in shelters for the homeless, worked as a day labourer, for example as a dishwasher at a chic hotel in Paris, and went hop-picking in Kent. It was during this time that Orwell developed the foundations of his narrative technique. The starting point is his own experience, the immersion of his own body in what is to be explored and portrayed. *Down and Out in Paris and London* is the first major result of this method. Orwell opens with a description of a morning street scene:

> The rue du Coq d'Or, Paris, seven in the morning. A succession of furious, choking yells from the street. Madame Monce, who kept the little hotel opposite mine, had come out on to the pavement to address a lodger on the third floor. Her bare feet were stuck into sabots and her grey hair was streaming down.

> *Madame Monce:* 'Sacrée salope! How many times have I told you not to squash bugs on the wallpaper? Do you think you've bought the hotel, eh? Why can't you throw them out of the window like everyone else? *Espèce de traînée!*
>
> *The woman on the third floor:* 'Va donc, eh! vieille vache!'
>
> Thereupon a whole variegated chorus of yells, as windows were flung open on every side and half the street joined in the quarrel. They shut up abruptly ten minutes later, when a squadron of cavalry rode past and people stopped shouting to look at them.
>
> I sketch this scene, just to convey something of the spirit of the rue du Coq d'Or. Not that quarrels were the only thing that happened there – but still, we seldom got through the morning without at least one outburst of this description. Quarrels, and the desolate cries of street hawkers, and the shouts of children chasing orange-peel over the cobbles, and at night loud singing and the sour reek of the refuse-carts, made up the atmosphere of the street (Orwell 2001 [1933]: 1).

This opening already shows the determining stylistic and narrative principle of the entire book: polyphony and juxtaposition. The individual voices rise from and are lost in the noise of daily life or are traced and individualised into single voices that tell stories and fates, which in turn lead to other stories, other fates. *Down and Out* consists of a collage of such small scenes, which function like narrative vignettes, descriptions of sounds and smells, brief reflections and portraits of individual people. It draws a panorama of diverse narratives about poverty, put forward by many contrasting voices; the voice of the first-person narrator is only one of them. The book does not merely portray the poor, as London did in *The People of the Abyss*, but it develops a method of letting them *speak for themselves*, and weaves a fabric of many stories, interrelated in various ways, which are, as the narrator says at one point, 'all part of the story' (ibid.).

This is where the eminently political aspect of this book resides: in the mediation and interconnection of perspectives towards a 'multi-perspectivity'. And this sets a process in motion in the reader that leads to perception, understanding and cognition.

The narrative of the first part of *Down and Out* is loosely organised around the perspectives of various characters including Boris, an unemployed waiter and former officer in the Belarusian army, whom the first-person narrator meets in chapter IV. In the second part of the book, the narrative emanates essentially from the first-person narrator; what is told is what he encounters on his way as a tramp in and around London. The two parts of the book are only thinly connected, and *Down and Out in Paris and London* remains a collage of narrative vignettes of varying length. The deficiency in narrative technique here is not merely a matter of artistic craftsmanship. It has its counterpart in a deficit of experience. In the last sentences of the book, Orwell admits: 'At present I do not feel that I have seen more than the fringe of poverty. ... That is a beginning' (ibid: 230). He continues:

> My story ends here. It is a fairly trivial story, and I can only hope that it has been interesting in the same way as a travel diary is interesting. I can at least say, Here is the world that awaits you if you are ever penniless. Some days I want to explore that world more thoroughly. I should like to know people like Mario and Paddy and Bill the moocher, not from casual encounters, but intimately; I should like to understand what really goes on in the souls of *plongeurs* and tramps and Embankment sleepers. *At present I do not feel that I have seen more than the fringe of poverty.*
>
> Still I can point to one or two things I have definitely learned by being hard up. I shall never again think that all tramps are drunken scoundrels, nor expect a beggar to be grateful when I give him a penny, nor be surprised if men out of work lack energy, nor subscribe to the Salvation Army, nor pawn my clothes, nor refuse a handbill, nor enjoy a meal at a smart restaurant. That is a beginning (ibid, emphasis by the author).

That was about to change – profoundly – with Orwell's fifth book *The Road to Wigan Pier*.

'WHAT I HAVE MOST WANTED TO DO ... IS TO MAKE POLITICAL WRITING INTO AN ART'

In 'Why I write', a short essay published in 1946 and at the same time a miniature autobiography, Orwell writes:

> What I have most wanted to do throughout the past ten years is to make political writing into an art. My starting point is always a feeling of partisanship, a sense of injustice. When I sit down to write a book, I do not say to myself, 'I am going to produce a work of art.' I write it because there is some lie that I want to expose, some fact to which I want to draw attention, and my initial concern is to get a hearing. But I could not do the work of writing a book, or even a long magazine article, if it were not also an aesthetic experience. Anyone who cares to examine my work will see that even when it is downright propaganda it contains much that a full-time politician would consider irrelevant (Orwell 1968 [1946a]: 6).

In January 1936, Orwell submitted his novel *Keep the Aspidistra Flying* to his publisher Victor Gollancz, who shortly afterwards commissioned him to write a book about mass unemployment and living conditions in the North of England. Without further ado, Orwell quit his job at the bookshop Booklover's Corner, in Hampstead, north London, and his flat and immediately set off to travel around the North of England. Orwell's stay in the industrial centres of the West Midlands, Yorkshire and Lancashire was to last two months and to change fundamentally his perspective on life as well as his writing. The result, *The Road to Wigan Pier*, marks the turning point in Orwell's entire *œuvre*: in this book, a masterpiece of the long-essay form, one can observe for the first time that concentrated, experience-saturated grasp of the things of the world – in the form of social reportage – and of thought – in the form of critique of ideology – for which Orwell was later to become world famous. *The Road to Wigan Pier* is the first book of Orwell's in which he pushed his political writing to the point where it really became an art form. The rhapsodic, meandering narrative form of *Down and Out in Paris and London* is elaborated in *The Road to Wigan Pier* into a dense account that grasps the individual phenomena in their larger social context, traces them down to the details of their effects on families and individuals, and, in constant recourse to the background and (pre-)judgement of the readership, evaluates them in terms of their overall social significance.

In chapter II of *The Road to Wigan Pier* – it is the most frequently quoted chapter in the book – Orwell describes the miners' daily work and the conditions underground. Perhaps most impressive are the sections in which Orwell describes how much effort and pain it takes to get to the miners' actual place of work, the coal-mining area hundreds of metres or kilometres underground. The journey by cage lift into the depths is only the smallest and by far the easiest part of the journey. What is really hard and exhausting are the distances that have to be covered horizontally below ground, in corridors that are so low that you can only cross them bent over or on all fours:

> At the start to walk stooping is rather a joke, but it is a joke that soon wears off. I am handicapped by being exceptionally tall, but when the roof falls to four feet or less it is a tough job for anybody except a dwarf or a child. You not only have to bend double, you have also got to keep your head up all the while so as to see the beams and girders and dodge them when they come. You have, therefore, a constant crick in the neck, but this is nothing to the pain in your knees and thighs. After half a mile it becomes (I am not exaggerating) an unbearable

PAPER

agony. You begin to wonder whether you will ever get to the end – still more, how on earth you are going to get back. Your pace grows slower and slower. You come to a stretch of a couple of hundred yards where it is all exceptionally low and you have to work yourself along in a squatting position. Then suddenly the roof opens out to a mysterious height – scene of an old fall of rock, probably – and for twenty whole yards you can stand upright. The relief is overwhelming. But after this there is another low stretch of a hundred yards and then a succession of beams which you have to crawl under. You go down on all fours; even this is a relief after the squatting business. But when you come to the end of the beams and try to get up again, you find that your knees have temporarily struck work and refuse to lift you. You call a halt, ignominiously, and say that you would like to rest for a minute or two. Your guide (a miner) is sympathetic. He knows that your muscles are not the same as his. 'Only another four hundred yards,' he says encouragingly; you feel that he might as well say another four hundred miles. But finally you do somehow creep as far as the coal face. You have gone a mile and taken the best part of an hour; a miner would do it in not much more than twenty minutes. Having got there, you have to sprawl in the coal dust and get your strength back for several minutes before you can even watch the work in progress with any kind of intelligence (Orwell 2014 [1937]: 23).

The immersion effect is achieved here through a detailed, gradual narration of the movements and the adversities they are subjected to under the conditions prevailing in the mine, in tandem with explanations of the various physical effects that gradually set in (walking bent over – back pain – suddenly being able to stand upright – relief – having to crawl on all fours – knee pain, etc.). The length of the sentences varies according to the movements, which become progressively heavier and more painful, and thus, on the one hand, reflects their physical sequence via the grammatical units of the sentence corpus, which are separated by a whole spectrum of perfectly placed and varied punctuations (dots, commas, semicolons, dashes, parentheses).

The account is, moreover, written in an 'oral' style: in other words, as it is written here, one might also hear it told in person, face-to-face. Interpolated parentheses such as '(I am not exaggerating)' serve both to attract the reader's attention as well as to emphasise what is being described ('an unbearable agony').

The passage quoted is a textbook case of the deceptive simplicity of Orwell's plain style. In fact, Orwell employs highly artful linguistic devices and narrative strategies to make the text interact dynamically with the reader, orienting the reader's perception and gradually organising his or her thinking towards a certain realisation (see Saunders 2008; Cain 2007; Fowler 1995). Orwell's aim is to convey the unimaginable physical exertions to which a miner is subjected, exertions that are exhausting even for a miner but unbearable for a normal person.

Yet these physical demands are not even part of the actual work of a miner – they only arise for him *on the way to and from his place of work*, where the very hard physical (and moreover extremely dangerous) work for which he is paid only *begins*.

> But what I want to emphasize is this. Here is this frightful business of crawling to and fro, which to any normal person is a hard day's work in itself; and it is not part of the miner's work at all, it is merely an extra, like the City man's daily ride in the Tube. The miner does that journey to and fro, and sandwiched in between there are seven and a half hours of savage work. I have never travelled much more than a mile to the coal face; but often it is three miles, in which case I and most people other than coal miners would never get there at all. This is the kind of point that one is always liable to miss. When you think of the coal-mine you think of depth, heat, darkness, blackened figures hacking at walls of coal; you don't think, necessarily, of those miles of creeping to and fro. There is the question of time, also. A miner's working shift of seven and a half hours does not sound very long, but one has got to add on to it at least an hour a day for 'travelling', more often two hours and sometimes three. Of course, the 'travelling' is not technically work and the miner is not paid for it; but it is as like work as makes no difference (Orwell 2014 [1937]: 25).

Orwell's real aim, here, is to show what is actually *outside* the horizon of experience – his own and that of the readers – and will always remain there, outside our horizon of experience: the actual work of a miner. Orwell's page-long detailed description of the physical exertions that an ordinary person simply cannot endure thus has the essential purpose of conveying an idea of how far the worlds of the miner and that of the reader – presumably belonging to the middle to upper classes – are actually separated from each other. Such a fundamental difference cannot simply be expressed; it must be *experienced* in its concrete meanings and consequences. The narrative is, therefore, concerned with conveying a sense of it to the reader, narrating it in as many of its characteristics as possible.

This work of mediation and interconnection pervades *The Road to Wigan Pier*. This becomes particularly clear when Orwell finally comes to talk about the actual work of the miners:

> Even when you watch the process of coal-extraction you probably only watch it for a short time, and it is not until you begin making a few calculations that you realize what a stupendous task the 'fillers' are performing. Normally each man has to clear a space four or five yards wide. The cutter has undermined the coal to the depth of five feet, so that if the seam of coal is three or four feet high, each man has to cut out, break up and load on to the belt something between seven and twelve cubic yards of coal. This is to say, taking a cubic yard as weighing twenty-seven hundred-weight, that each man is shifting coal at a speed approaching two tons an hour. I have just enough experience of pick and shovel work to be able to grasp what this means. When I am digging trenches in my garden, if I shift two tons of earth during the afternoon, I feel that I have earned my tea. But earth is tractable stuff compared with coal, and I don't have to work kneeling down, a thousand feet underground, in suffocating heat and swallowing coal dust with every breath I take; nor do I have to walk a mile bent double before I begin. The miner's job would be as much beyond my power as it would be to perform on a flying trapeze or to win the Grand National. I am not a manual labourer and please God I never shall be one, but there are some kinds of manual work that I could do if I had to. At a pinch I could be a tolerable road-sweeper or an inefficient gardener or even a tenth-rate farm hand. But by no conceivable amount of effort or training could I become a coal-miner, the work would kill me in a few weeks (Orwell 2014 [1937]: 28).

When Orwell narrates the living conditions of the miners and their work, which produces the raw material needed for all energy production (at that time), he also tells of the material basis of our civilisation, so remote from the toil of the miner and yet so dependent on it:

> More than anyone else, perhaps, the miner can stand as the type of the manual worker, not only because his work is so exaggeratedly awful, but also because *it is so vitally necessary and yet so remote from our experience*, so invisible, as it were, that we are capable of forgetting it as we forget the blood in our veins (ibid 30; emphasis by the author).

AUTOBIOGRAPHICAL RESEARCH AND CLASS ANALYSIS

In the second half of *The Road to Wigan Pier* (chapters VIII to XIII), Orwell reflects on the development of his political views and his bourgeois upbringing, thus also on the background against which the living conditions of the workers always present themselves to him – and hence to the reader – in a certain light, through a certain filter. Orwell's examination of his social conditioning leads him to the analysis of the class from which he comes. He calls it the 'lower-upper-middle class' (ibid: 113).

At the beginning of his expeditions into the social 'underworld', Orwell clings to the illusion of being able to overcome class boundaries. His first expedition into the London slums seemed to him like a kind of adventure – to rid him of his social origins and class conditioning:

> [I]t is that first expedition that sticks most vividly in my mind, because of the strangeness of it – the strangeness of being at last down there among 'the lowest of the low', and on terms of utter equality with working-class people. A tramp, it is true, is not a typical working-class person; still, when you are among tramps you are at any rate merged in one section – one sub-caste – of the working class, a thing which so far as I know can happen to you in no other way. For several days I wandered through the northern outskirts of London with an Irish tramp. I was his mate, temporarily. We shared the same cell at night, and he told me the history of his life and I told him a fictitious history of mine, and we took it in turns to beg at likely-looking houses and divided up the proceeds. I was very happy. Here I was, among 'the lowest of the low', at the bedrock of the Western world! The class-bar was down, or seemed to be down. *And down there in the squalid and, as a matter of fact, horribly boring sub-world of the tramp I had a feeling of release, of adventure, which seems absurd when I look back, but which was sufficiently vivid at the time* (ibid: 142, emphasis by the author).

Life in the social netherworld, however, is not a romantic adventure story that leads to the dissolution of boundaries and brings freedom but turns out to be an exhausting struggle with the tiniest, most mundane things, hard and dull at the same time. To have some experience of life 'down and out' and to establish personal relationships with workers or tramps does not mean overcoming class boundaries, but only getting a closer look at and a better idea of the class problem: 'But unfortunately you do not solve the class problem by making friends with tramps. At most you get rid of some of your own class-prejudice by doing so' (ibid: 143).

DOMINIC ANGELOCH

For some months I lived entirely in coal-miners' houses. I ate my meals with the family, I washed at the kitchen sink, I shared bedrooms with miners, drank beer with them, played darts with them, talked to them by the hour together. But though I was among them, and I hope and trust they did not find me a nuisance, I was not one of them, and they knew it even better than I did. However much you like them, however interesting you find their conversation, there is always that accursed itch of class-difference, like the pea under the princess's mattress. It is not a question of dislike or distaste, only of *difference*, but it is enough to make real intimacy impossible (ibid: 145, italics in the original).

To a member of the upper classes, the world of the workers and the poor, although it literally begins at his doorstep, is so invisible that in order to understand its social conditions at least halfway, he has to explore it like a biologist explores the habitat of an as yet undiscovered species on a distant island. However, once he has exposed himself to this world and to the experience of what life in it means, he understands that the social 'under-world' is really nothing more than a certain part of the one human world in which we all live. For him, one boundary after another begins to fall: what was previously unimaginable is now normal, what was previously unthinkable becomes an integral part of one's perspective. And yet some demarcations remain – despite all experiences, despite all efforts. And Orwell names these demarcations as the border between the classes: 'Whichever way you turn this curse of class-difference confronts you like a wall of stone. Or rather it is not so much like a stone wall as the plate-glass pane of an aquarium; it is so easy to pretend that it isn't there, and so impossible to get through it' (ibid).

The border between the classes may be invisible, but it cannot really be overcome. 'Unfortunately it is nowadays the fashion to pretend that the glass is penetrable. Of course everyone knows that class-prejudice exists, but at the same time everyone claims that he, in some mysterious way, is exempt from it' (ibid: 146). This is one of the essential insights Orwell drew from his years of experience with the world of workers and the poor. It was – and can be only – gained from experience.

It is, however, in the nature of experience that one cannot plan it, just as one cannot plan the insights that result from it. Experience means, among other things, destroying assumptions and perceptions and seeing entire world views gradually or suddenly deprived of their foundation. In this respect, all experiences are unpleasant and painful; one does not actually 'make' them – in the sense of an activity, a producing or manufacturing – one rather *suffers* them.

As the German philosopher Otto Friedrich Bollnow writes on the question of what experience actually is:

> In experience, man is at the mercy of what comes upon him. The experiences invade him. He cannot defend himself against them. Nor can he determine the time of the experiences. He has to take them when they come and how they come. The only thing he can do … is to expose himself to the possibility of the experiences, that is, to put himself in danger. … The experiences one has are always painful experiences. Experiences are always unpleasant. Pleasant experiences do not exist. … This assertion may sound very idiosyncratically pointed. But only because one has become jaded by the washed-out use of the word. … The important thing for us is that the deeply felt painfulness draws attention to the essence of experience, to the inner structure of the process in which we have experiences (Bollnow 1974: 20; author's translation).

With experience comes risk, and often enough tangible danger, even if it is only to our previous thinking, which has to be subjected to a revision that sometimes has psychologically catastrophic effects. This is what the British psychoanalyst Wilfred Bion called 'catastrophic change' (see Bion 1965, chapter 1; Bion 2007 [1970], chapters 11 and 12): every new thought is perceived by the psyche as potentially disruptive and upsetting; enduring this upheaval and integrating the new thought into the psyche leads to growth, but this challenge of integration, like growth, is a painful process that depends on the individual's ability to resist the associated doubts, fear and mental fragmentation.

The essence of experience in the first place is that something goes or has gone completely differently from what was expected, and the task posed by the adverse experiences one has had is that one must be able to deal with them practically and somehow integrate them into one's thinking. 'Every experience worthy of the name thwarts an expectation,' writes the hermeneuticist Hans-Georg Gadamer (1960: 338; author's translation). But not every disappointed expectation is already an experience; experience is rather a response to this thwarted expectation, the abandonment of a previously assumed position and the restoration of a meaningful order in a new position. One does not merely *have* experiences, one *lives through them*.

CONCLUSION

This is the background and the real subject of *Down and Out in Paris and London* and *The Road to Wigan Pier* as well as Orwell's subsequent book *Homage to Catalonia* (Orwell 2013 [1938]). They are all books about experiences that Orwell actively sought out and exposed himself to, but found each time and in every detail quite different from what he had planned, wished for or hoped for, had completely different experiences from what was foreseeable, from which completely different insights followed than had been thought. Not only did he endure the associated questioning of all previous certainties, but he also pursued it specifically in the interest of exploring what really is.[4]

Under the hand of a lesser author than Orwell, they would have become reports of experiences, travelogues, perhaps even adventure stories. Orwell's books, however, are the works they are because they contain the experiences on which they are based, embedded in form and content. As Peter Davison writes on *Down and Out* and *The Road to Wigan Pier*:

> He was ill-prepared politically and socially for what he was to be faced with. Both books reveal a learning process presented in such a way that the reader is taken through the experiences described. It is that personal exploration and the expression of those gut-reactions, the appeal to 'decency' (so important a concept for Orwell) that lifts these books out of their time (Davison 1996: 81).

With these books and his later essays and journalism, Orwell completely redefined the literary form of the essay as a text on the borderline between autobiography, narrative, social reportage, theory, (pop) cultural and social criticism. Moreover, characteristic of a new form of storytelling created by Orwell is to present experiences: Orwell's texts allow the reader to live through the narrated experiences in the act of reading, to experience while reading. Orwell's texts *narrate* experiences and *convey* them at the same time.

NOTES

[1] Reliable and helpful accounts of Orwell's life and work are to be found e.g. in: Shelden 1991 and Peter Davison 1996. Particularly recommended is the compilation *A Life in Letters* (Orwell 2010). There (pp 493–503) also a detailed timetable of the most important events in Orwell's life

[2] See Orwell 1968 [1948], and Orwell 1968 [1939], as well as Booth (1902–03). See also: Trilling 1986

[3] An illuminating portrait of Jack London is drawn by Orwell in Orwell 1968 [1945a]

[4] According to his friend Tosco Fyvel, Orwell's 'crucial experience' was the process of becoming the author he wanted to be, through long periods of poverty, failure and humiliation of all kinds: 'His crucial experience ... was his struggle to turn himself into a writer, one which led through long periods of poverty, failure and humiliation, and about which he has written almost nothing directly. The sweat and agony was less in the slum-life than in the effort to turn the experience into literature' (Fyvel 1956: 257; see also Fyvel 1982: 48)

REFERENCES

Beadle, Gordon B. (1978) George Orwell's literary studies of poverty in England, *Twentieth Century Literature*, Vol. 24, No. 2 pp 188-201

Benjamin, Walter (1968 [1936]) The storyteller: Reflections on the works of Nikolai Leskov. In *Illuminations*, trans by Zohn, H., New York: Harcourt Brace Jovanovich pp 83-109

Bion, Wilfred (2007 [1970]) *Attention and Interpretation*, London: Karnac

Bion, Wilfred (1965) *Transformations: Change from Learning to Growth*, London: Karnac

Bollnow, Otto Friedrich (1974) Was ist Erfahrung? [What is experience?] Vente, R. E. (ed.) *Erfahrung und Erfahrungswissenschaft* [*Experience and Empirical Science*], Stuttgart pp 19-29

Booth, Charles (1902-1903) *The Life and Labour of the People of London*, 17 vols., London: Hutchinson

Cain, William E. (2007) Orwell's essays as a literary experience, Rodden, John (ed.) *The Cambridge Companion to George Orwell*, Cambridge: Cambridge University Press pp 76-86

Carey, John (2003) The invisible man, *The Sunday Times*, 18 May p. 35

Davison, Peter (1996) *George Orwell. A Literary Life*, London: Macmillan Press

Davison, Peter (2001) Introduction, *Orwell and the Dispossessed*, Harmondsworth: Penguin pp ix-xv

Fowler, Roger (1995) *The Language of George Orwell*, Hampshire, London: Macmillan Press

Fyvel, Tosco R. (1956) *A Case for George Orwell? Twentieth Century*, Vol. 9

Fyvel, Tosco R. (1982) *George Orwell: A Personal Memoir*, London: Macmillan

Gadamer, Hans-Georg (1960) *Wahrheit und Methode: Grundzüge einer philosophischen Hermeneutik* [*Truth and Method: Outlines of a Philosophical Hermeneutics*], Tübingen: Mohr Siebeck

Iser, Wolfgang (1994 [1976]) *Der Akt des Lesens* [*The Act of Reading*], München: UTB

Jacobson, Dan (1971) Orwell's slumming. Gross, Miriam (ed.) *The World of George Orwell*, New York: Weidenfeld and Nicolson pp 48-52

London, Jack (1998) *The Call of the Wild, White Fang & To Build a Fire* (Modern Library Classics), Introduction by Doctorow, E. L., London: Penguin

London, Jack (1982 [1903]) *The People of the Abyss*, in: *Novels and Social Writings: The People of the Abyss / The Road / The Iron Heel / Martin Eden / John Barleycorn* (Library of America #7. Jack London Edition Vol. 2), New York: Library of America pp 1-184

Orwell, George (2001 [1933]) *Down and Out in Paris and London*. London: Penguin

Orwell, George (2014 [1937]), *The Road to Wigan Pier*, London: Penguin

Orwell, George (2013 [1938]) *Homage to Catalonia*, London: Penguin

Orwell, George (1968 [1939]) Charles Dickens, Orwell, Sonia, and Angus Ian (eds) *The Collected Essays, Journalism and Letters of George Orwell, Vol. 1: An Age Like This 1920-1940*, London: Secker & Warburg pp 413-460

Orwell, George (1968 [1942]) Rudyard Kipling, Orwell, Sonia, and Angus Ian (eds) *The Collected Essays, Journalism and Letters of George Orwell, Vol. 2: My Country Right or Left 1940-1943*, London: Secker & Warburg pp 184-197

Orwell, George (1968 [1945a]), Introduction to 'Love and life and other stories' by Jack London, Orwell, Sonia, and Angus Ian (eds) *The Collected Essays, Journalism and Letters of George Orwell, Vol. 4: In Front of Your Nose 1945-1950*, London: Secker & Warburg pp 23-29

DOMINIC ANGELOCH

Orwell, George (1968 [1945b]) Good bad books, Orwell, Sonia, and Angus Ian (eds) *The Collected Essays, Journalism and Letters of George Orwell*, Vol. 4: *In Front of Your Nose 1945-1950*, London: Secker & Warburg pp 19-22

Orwell, George (1968 [1946a]) Why I write, Orwell, Sonia, and Angus Ian (eds) *The Collected Essays, Journalism and Letters of George Orwell. Vol. 1: An Age Like This 1920-1940*, London: Secker & Warburg pp 1-7

Orwell, George (1968 [1946b]) In front of your nose, Orwell, Sonia, and Angus Ian (ed.) *The Collected Essays, Journalism and Letters of George Orwell, Vol. 4: In Front of Your Nose 1945-1950*, London: Secker & Warburg pp 122-125

Orwell, George (1968 [1948]) George Gissing, Orwell, Sonia, and Angus Ian (eds) *The Collected Essays, Journalism and Letters of George Orwell, Vol. 4: In Front of Your Nose 1945-1950*, London: Secker & Warburg pp 428-436

Orwell, George (2010) *A Life in Letters*, selected and annotated by Peter Davison, London: Penguin

Perkins, Marianne (1992) *The Politics of Poverty: George Orwell's* Down and Out in Paris and London, MA thesis at the University of Texas. Available online at https://digital.library.unt.edu/ark:/67531/metadc500674/, accessed on 5 August 2022

Sabin, Margery (2007) The truths of experience: Orwell's nonfiction of the 1930s, Rodden, John (ed.) *The Cambridge Companion to George Orwell*, Cambridge: Cambridge University Press pp 76-86

Saunders, Loraine (2008) *The Unsung Artistry of George Orwell: The Novels from* Burmese Days *to* Nineteen Eighty-Four, London: Routledge

Shelden, Michael (1991) *Orwell. The Authorised Biography*, London, Melbourne, Auckland: Heinemann

Trilling, Lionel (1986) George Orwell and the politics of truth, Bloom, Harold (ed.) *George Orwell (Modern Critical Views)*, New York, New Haven, Philadelphia: Chelsea House pp 35-46

NOTE ON THE CONTRIBUTOR

PD Dr Dominic Angeloch (angeloch@lingua.uni-frankfurt.de) is *Privatdozent* for General and Comparative Literature at the Goethe-University, Frankfurt am Main, and Managing Editor of the German monthly psychoanalytic journal, *Psyche*. He received his doctorate from the LMU Munich with a thesis on the methodology of psychoanalytic aesthetics and Gustave Flaubert. He gained his postdoctoral qualitification, the *Habilitation*, in 2020, at the University of Frankfurt am Main with a thesis investigating the conditions of the transformation of experience into literature and of literature into experience in Wilfred Bion's and George Orwell's œuvres. In the spring of 2022, he had published *Die Wahrheit schreiben. George Orwell: Entwicklung und Methode seines Schreibens* [*Writing the Truth: The Development of George Orwell's Method of Narration*] (Edition Tiamat, Berlin). For a list of publications and activities, see: https://www.uni-frankfurt.de/85325555/PD_Dr__Dominic_Angeloch.

The Elephant in the Room: Reassessing the Genre of George Orwell's 'Shooting an elephant'

Carol Biederstadt reflects on the implications of the parallels between Orwell's 'Shooting an elephant' and several of the works of Reginald Campbell.

In my article 'Orwellian or Campbellian? "Invisible sources" in Orwell's "Shooting an elephant" and *Burmese Days*' (2020), I set forth the hypothesis that Reginald Campbell's memoir *Teak Wallah* (1935) and several of his previously published fictional works may have influenced Orwell's celebrated essay 'Shooting an elephant' (1936) and his novel *Burmese Days* (1934). Since then, I have discussed the idea with Orwell scholars, Thai history experts, colleagues and students. Without fail, the idea that Orwell may have plagiarised – or at least the impression that I may be suggesting he did! – has entered each discussion. Such conclusions, however, not only miss the mark, but also draw attention away from the more significant implications of my argument.

All writers draw on the works of others to some degree and, occasionally, the ethics of influence come into question. One much publicised case, for example, involved a copyright infringement suit brought against writer Alex Haley, author of the best-selling and Pulitzer Prize-winning novel *Roots* (1976). Haley was, in fact, twice accused of plagiarism. Although the first case, brought by Margaret Walker Alexander, author of the novel *Jubilee* (1966), was dismissed in 1977, Haley was again accused when Harold Courlander, author of the novel *The African* (1967), filed a case against him in 1978 (Lubasch 1978). In question were a whopping 81 similar passages between *Roots* and *The African* (Lescaze et al. 1978), and Haley eventually conceded that three of those passages, the most damning of which was 'Yooo-hooo-ah-hooo, don't you hear me calling you?', had come from Courlander's novel. Representing a plantation slave field call, the same line, including the distinctive spelling, had appeared in *The African* nine years earlier (Lubasch 1978). The case was eventually settled out of court, with Haley agreeing to pay Courlander $650,000 and his attorneys issuing the following statement: 'Alex Haley acknowledges and regrets that various materials from *The African* by Harold Courlander found their way into his book *Roots*' (Kaplan 2016). Haley evidently recognised that the similarities between passages in his own and Courlander's works were so great that his chances of prevailing in the case were slim. Though they include nothing as damaging as Haley's use of the 'Yooo-hooo-ah-hooo' line, Orwell's 'Shooting an elephant' and *Burmese Days* contain numerous elements of plot, theme and even language that resemble those found in the works of Reginald Campbell. In many instances, the degree of similarity is comparable to that found in passages Courlander objected to in Haley's *Roots* (see, for example: Lescaze et al. 1978 and Biederstadt 2020). Lest Orwell's intellectual integrity comes into question, however, it is important to note that these cases differ in significant ways.

For one, even if Orwell did appropriate elements of Campbell's writings, the textual interplay between the two writers was almost certainly not what either would have considered 'plagiarism' since Orwell so thoroughly transformed any borrowed ideas and made them uniquely his own. Indeed, throughout his career, Orwell was known to absorb the themes of others. It is well documented, for instance, that Orwell was influenced by the works of Jonathan Swift, Jack London and Somerset Maugham. Similarities between *Nineteen Eighty-Four* and Yevgeny Zamyatin's novel *We* (1924) have been widely discussed (see, for example, Deutscher 1971 [1955]: 30-35), and it is generally accepted that Orwell's famous 'All animals are equal' line was inspired by Philip Guedalla's short story 'A Russian fairy tale' (1930) about a Good Fairy 'who believed that all fairies were equal before the law, but held strongly that some fairies were more equal than others' (see Patai 1984: 309).[1]

In addition to these well-documented influences and borrowings, numerous examples of what Jonathan Rose (1992) has labelled 'invisible sources' – works by writers who likely influenced Orwell but whom he never specifically mentioned in his writing – have also been identified. Daphne Patai, for example, notes the novel's resemblance to *Swastika Night* (1937) by Katharine Burdekin (Murray Constantine), stating: 'There is no direct evidence that Orwell was acquainted with Burdekin's novel; only the internal similarities between *Nineteen Eighty-Four* and *Swastika Night* … suggest a connection' (1984: 254). Likewise, Rose refers to the similarities between *Nineteen Eighty-Four* and the works of Olaf Stapledon and Alfred Noyes (1992: 132-136). Still, none of these examples of intertextuality in any way suggest that Orwell's works involve plagiarism. As Rose explains:

> Orwell had the kind of genius that can construct a classic novel by borrowing and refashioning elements of ephemeral literature. He had been reading dystopian tales since boyhood, always noting what worked and what didn't – the sort of technical criticism one would expect from someone on the lookout for reusable ideas. ... He cannibalised the best bits of Zamyatin, H. G. Wells, James Burnham and any number of other authors. If he did the same with Stapledon, he put an original spin on everything he borrowed (1992: 135-136).

Rose's comments about Orwell's 'borrowing and refashioning' of the works of others and his conjecture about the likely influence of the works of Stapledon and other 'invisible sources' could as easily be applied to the works of Reginald Campbell.

Furthermore, there is no indication that Campbell was aggrieved about any similarities between Orwell's works and his own. Admittedly, unlike the case of Courlander vs Haley, no conclusive evidence has to date surfaced to prove that Campbell was aware of Orwell or his essay 'Shooting an elephant' or novel *Burmese Days*. Orwell was still a fledgling writer at the time the texts in question were written and, without doubt, Campbell was by far the more famous writer in the early to mid-1930s. Indeed, even in 1988, in reference to the 1986 'Oxford in Asia' paperback re-issue of Campbell's *Teak Wallah*, writer and journalist James Fallows put forth the opinion: 'This is a marvelous book, which should be better known than George Orwell's *Burmese Days*' (1988: 92). Nevertheless, both Orwell and Campbell had returned to and were writing in England by that time, and at least some tenuous connection between the two is conceivable if not probable.

Moreover, Campbell lived until 1950 – long enough to learn of Orwell's rising star – yet even so, no evidence seems to suggest that Campbell ever cried foul. On the contrary, Campbell made the curious decision to assign the uncommon pseudonym 'Orwell' to Harry L. Norman, the heroic figure repeatedly referred to in his memoir *Teak Wallah* (Wattananikorn 2018: 159, 162 and 2019), a fact that makes the similarities in the works of Campbell and Orwell even more compelling. Could Campbell's use of the name 'Orwell' have been a vaguely concealed acknowledgement – a sort of inside joke? Perhaps. But if so, it would hardly suggest that Campbell was offended by the similarities between Orwell's works and his own. Norman was a man Campbell held in highest esteem, after all, so if anything, the deliberate use of Orwell's name may indicate that Campbell had been flattered by the imitation of a young writer of Orwell's calibre.

CAROL BIEDERSTADT

As riveting as it may be to speculate, however, such conjecture should not come at the expense of ignoring the real 'elephant' in the room: that the significance of an Orwell-Campbell connection lies in the way such a link affects perception of the genre of 'Shooting an elephant'. For sure, scholarly opinion of the essay has long been divided. In one camp are those such as Maung Htin Aung (1970: 27) and Stephen Ingle (1996: 11), who clearly view the essay as autobiographical. More recently, Gerry Abbott, drawing on poems written by Orwell and the autobiography of Captain H. R. Robinson, also argued that Orwell did, indeed, shoot an elephant (2016: 116-122). And in 2021 Jeffrey Meyers wrote that as a policeman in Burma, Orwell 'killed a valuable elephant, after it had calmed down and was no longer dangerous, to display his power and save face as a colonial official' (2021: 21), while Orwell's son, Richard Blair, speculating on why his father appears to have done no gardening in Burma, surmised: 'Perhaps in real life Orwell was too busy shooting elephants and hanging miscreants!' (2021: 10).

In the other camp are those such as D. C. R. A. Goonetilleke, who points out that, although Orwell's Burma essays are 'universally lauded as autobiographical', they may not be so at all (1982: 183). Bernard Crick, for example, is famously said to have doubted the veracity of the reportage, spurring the rebuke of Sonia Orwell, his second wife: 'Of course he shot a fucking elephant. He said he did. Why do you always doubt his fucking word!' (Barnes 2009). In *George Orwell: A Life,* however, Crick explains that it was then fashionable to write in an 'ambiguous, first-person descriptive vein … which blurred any clear line between fiction and autobiography – truthful to experiences but not necessarily to fact' (1982 [1980]: 166). Similarly, while conceding the debate surrounding the issue, Peter Davison, editor of the 20-volume *Complete Works of George Orwell* (*CWGO*), originally seemed convinced that Orwell had shot an elephant, citing the 'tape-recorded reminiscences of one of Orwell's colleagues in Burma, George Stuart' (*CWGO* X: 506). Yet in 2006, he amended his notes to the essay to include a reference to an article entitled 'Rogue elephant shot', which had appeared in a 1926 issue of *The Rangoon Gazette.* An account of a subdivisional officer who shot an elephant in Burma, the story bears many similarities to Orwell's essay, and while Davison offers no analysis, the implication that Orwell may have drawn inspiration from the case is clear (Davison 2006: 166). In his most recent study of Orwell, John Rodden, too, acknowledges that the genre of 'Shooting an elephant' has been the subject of much debate and suggests that the essay, like 'A hanging' (of 1931), may best be described as a work of 'faction' (2020: 80-83).

Only once does Orwell himself appear to have called the essay autobiographical. In a letter to William Maclellan, editor of *Million*, Orwell responded to a June 1945 article by J. E. Miller entitled 'George Orwell and our time'. The article had erroneously claimed that 'Shooting an elephant' was an extract from *Burmese Days*, and by way of clarification, Orwell wrote: 'There is no connection between the two pieces of writing named. "Shooting an elephant" is an autobiographical sketch published in 1936, and "Burmese Days" is a third-person novel published several years earlier' (Davison 2006: 107-108). How literally, though, should this one letter be taken? Should modern readers, as Sonia clearly did, take his word at face value?

Orwell once said that Charles Dickens was 'one of those writers who are well worth stealing' (1982 [1939]: 454). Could Campbell, with his knowledge of Southeast Asia, have also been 'one of those writers'? This question may never be definitively answered, but accepting the likelihood that Orwell was influenced by Campbell further undermines the argument that the essay is strictly autobiographical. Instead, although Orwell certainly draws on his experience as a police officer in Burma, the Campbell postulation would support the view that the text may, in fact, be a masterpiece of short fiction – or perhaps what Rodden has labelled 'faction'.

- The author would like to thank John Rodden for allowing her to access his work in progress.

NOTE

[1] John Rodden has written extensively about the similarities between *Nineteen Eighty-Four* and both Zamyatin's *We* and the contentious 'all animals are equal' line from *Animal Farm* (2011 and 2021).

REFERENCES

Abbott, Gerry (2016) The poet who wanted to shoot an elephant, *George Orwell Studies*, Vol. 1, No. 1 pp 116-123

Aung, Maung Htin (1970) George Orwell and Burma, *Asian Affairs*, Vol. 1, No. 1 pp 19-28

Barnes, Julian (2009) Such, such was Eric Blair, *The New York Review*, 12 March. Available online at https://www.nybooks.com/articles/2009/03/12/such-such-was-eric-blair/?lp_txn_id=1271989, accessed on 23 August 2021

Biederstadt, Carol (2020) Orwellian or Campbellian? 'Invisible sources' in Orwell's 'Shooting an elephant' and *Burmese Days*, *George Orwell Studies*, Vol. 4, No. 2 pp 45-63

Blair, Richard (2021) 'I have been too busy battling with the garden …' The Orwell Society *Journal*, No. 18 pp 9-12

Crick, Bernard (1982 [1980]) *George Orwell: A Life*, Harmondsworth: Penguin

Davison, Peter (1998) *The Complete Works of George Orwell, Vol. X: A Kind of Compulsion*, London: Secker & Warburg

Davison, Peter (2006) *The Lost Orwell*, London: Timewell Press

CAROL BIEDERSTADT

Deutscher, Isaac (1971) '1984' – The mysticism of cruelty, Hynes, Samuel (ed.) *Twentieth Century Interpretations of* 1984, Englewood Cliffs: Prentice Hall pp 29-40; first published in *Russia in Transition* (1957) New York: Coward-McCann and published in England as *Heretics and Renegades* (1955) London: Hamish Hamilton

Fallows, James (1988) When East met West, *The Atlantic*, September. Available online at https://www.theatlantic.com/magazine/archive/1988/09/when-east-met-west/668831/, accessed on 11 August 2022

Goonetilleke, D. C. R. A. (1982) George Orwell's *Burmese Days*: The novelist as reformer, *Kalyani: Journal of Humanities and Social Sciences of the University of Kelaniya*, Vol. 1, Nos 1-2 pp 182-194

Ingle, Stephen (1993) *George Orwell: A Political Life*, Manchester: Manchester University Press

Kaplan, Don (2016) Amazing 'Roots' returns after 40 years, dredging up Alex Haley plagiarism scandal, *The New York Daily News*, 19 May. Available online at www.nydailynews.com/entertainment/tv/amazing-roots-returns-dredging-plagiarism-scandal-article-1.2642946, accessed on 1 August 2021

Lescaze, Lee, Saperstein, Saundra and Kennedy, John (1978) Bethesda author settles 'Roots' suit for $500,000, *The Washington Post*, 15 December. Available online at https://www.washingtonpost.com/archive/politics/1978/12/15/bethesda-author-settles-roots-suit-for-500000/f97b693c-5336-46b3-8ab0-1b19856e8964/, accessed on 17 July 2021

Lubasch, Arnold H. (1978) 'Roots' plagiarism suit is settled, *The New York Times*, 15 December. Available online at *https://www.nytimes.com/1978/12/15/archives/roots-plagiarism-suit-is-settled-roots-plagiarism-suit-is-settled.html*, accessed on 17 July 2021

Meyers, Jeffrey (2021) The impact of Burma, The Orwell Society *Journal*, No. 18 pp 20-23

Orwell, George (1982 [1939]) Charles Dickens, *The Collected Essays, Journalism and Letters of George Orwell, Vol. 1: An Age Like This, 1920-1940*, London: Penguin pp 454-504

Patai, Daphne (1984) *The Orwell Mystique: A Study in Male Ideology*, Amherst: University of Massachusetts Press

Rodden, John (2011) *The Unexamined Orwell*, Austin: University of Texas

Rodden, John (2020) *Becoming George Orwell: Life and Letters, Legend and Legacy*, Princeton: Princeton University Press

Rodden, John (2021) Purloined prose? Borrowing, stealing, and the creative process, unpublished manuscript

Rose, Jonathan (1992) The invisible sources of *Nineteen Eighty-Four*, Rose, Jonathan (ed.) *The Revised Orwell*, East Lansing: Michigan State University pp 131-147

Wattananikorn, Kittichai (2018) *British Teak Wallahs in Northern Thailand from 1876-1956*, Bangkok: White Lotus

Wattananikorn, Kittichai (2019) Personal communication

NOTE ON THE CONTRIBUTOR

Carol Biederstadt is Associate Professor of English at Union College, in Cranford, New Jersey, USA.

ARTICLE

Retracing Orwell's Steps in Wigan – Balancing Curiosity with Respect

Timothy Foster, photographer and film-maker based in London, returned to his hometown, Wigan, some eighty years after Orwell ventured North to research the plight of the poor and unemployed. Here, he reflects on his experience.

In June 2016, the UK voted to leave the EU in a narrow vote of 51.9 per cent to 48.1 per cent. The campaigns for either side had been bitterly waged, with issues around free movement and immigration, notions of Britishness and questions of race and identity coming to the fore. In the wake of the fallout, in July 2016, I found myself sweating heavily and feeling lost. I had the idea to walk the length of the country, at this time of great disharmony and division, in order to discover, with my photographs, what we all had in common. I set off hopefully from East London for Romford with my rucksack – but all I found after my 15-mile trek across the North Circular was that Tudors apparently built loft conversions.

Another tack was in order – I got on the train back to my hometown of Wigan, exactly 80 years after Orwell himself ventured North to research *The Road to Wigan Pier*. In this, he documented the bleak living conditions experienced by the Depression-era working class of the area, giving voice to those he felt were being ignored by the establishment. Walking the streets of Wigan in 2016, I started to feel that, despite the passage of time, Orwell's words still deeply resonated and decided to retrace his steps. I had no idea that I would be walking those streets for the next 18 months. (Luckily, having once been a postman in Manchester, I am used to walking – as well as being attacked by the occasional three-legged Doberman: it's a long story).

I set out to uncover modern Wigan with the intention of wanting to laugh with – not at – its residents, unlike many journalists venturing North to shoot 'poverty porn', I've always had an affection for my hometown and was keen to balance my curiosity with respect. Despite this, at times I still felt like an outsider. I've been in many tricky situations as a photographer of two decades, including the time on an assignment in Los Angeles when two men

TIMOTHY FOSTER

pulled a gun on me and somehow I'd blagged my way out. And in my first week back in Wigan, a kid pointed a gun at me from a car window and the same tidal wave of fear poured over me. The kid smiled and in a knee-jerk reaction I took his photograph from the hip – realising, in that moment, that it was just a toy gun, and he was just a bored kid in a school-run traffic jam.

A lot has changed since my 20 years away from Wigan. More has changed since Orwell's – but the scars from the town's loss of its industrial heritage remain. After its boom time during the Industrial Revolution as a major mill and coal mining town – in 1926, Wigan, just one eighth size of London, had an incredible 72 mines – it suffered a slump from which it has never really recovered.

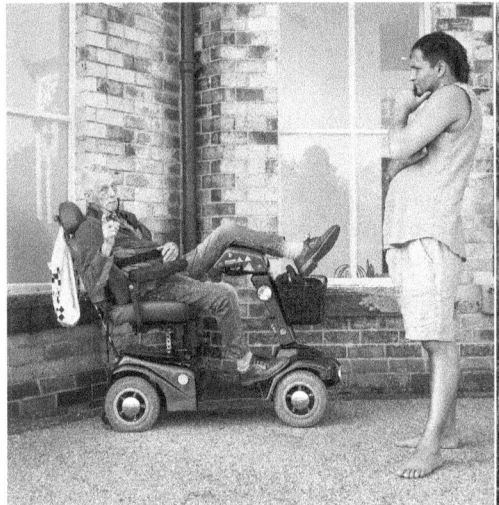 

Jonah and the 92 year old Alan - WiganWigan kids behind tree

Many Wiganers want to move away from this industrial past, alongside the accompanying enduring music hall joke that began with George Formby, who famously sang 'On the Wigan boat express', with the running gag that Wigan's famous 'pier' was an idyllic seaside paradise when, in fact, it was the end of a coal tramway running from a colliery and stretching over a muddy canal. Formby's song speaks to my hometown's resilient spirit: making a joke in the face of poverty and adversity – and being able to laugh at yourself. I call it the trauma of Post-Industrial Economic Stress, or P.I.E.S for short – a joke most Wiganers will understand.

Orwell's words on Wigan walked with me every day, especially his brutal, self-deprecating honesty. I photographically played with the then and now in a long conversation with him and his text that lasted 18 months and stretched to nearly 50,000 photographs. In 2017, these became my solo exhibition, 'All roads lead to Wigan Pier', at the Turnpike in Leigh. On the opening night, I found a man downstairs who was hesitant about coming upstairs to the show. 'It's full of them posh people,' he said. So I took him up myself and showed him around. Twenty minutes later he returned and presented me with a dandelion flower, and said: 'Thanks for making us exist.'

Wigan woman collapse

- All images are taken from *All Roads Lead to Wigan Pier*, Setanta Books, £25, by Timothy Foster and reproduced with his kind permission. See timothyfoster.co.uk. Timothy Foster gives Orwell Society George Talk: https://www.youtube.com/watch?v=miMknNY1lkc.

Authors and Titles Mentioned in *The Road to Wigan Pier*

L. J. Hurst

This is an attempt to tabulate all the references to authors and titles mentioned by George Orwell in *The Road to Wigan Pier* (1937). Where first names or titles are omitted by Orwell these are added in brackets; where a work is not a book it may be noted in parentheses such as '(play)' in the Greenwood reference; where an author is given without Orwell naming his work, but that work can be determined, the title is shown in brackets. Only ranks and titles used by Orwell are shown, such as 'Rev.', 'Professor' and 'Mr'. Groups of authors named without specific works are left as single grouped entries. There is no attempt at explaining why Orwell names or refers to any author or book.

Authors	Titles Mentioned
Rev. W. R. Inge	*England*[1]
	Colliery Year Book and Coal Trades Directory for 1935
Mr Joseph Jones	*The Coal Scuttle*
John Orr	[*Food Health and Income*]
[Hippolyte-Prosper-Olivier 'Lissa'] Lissagaray	*History of the Commune*[2]
[Walter] Greenwood (play)	*Love on the Dole*
Samuel Butler	*Way of All Flesh*
	Erewhon
Somerset Maugham	*On a Chinese Screen*
Professor [George] Saintsbury	*Second Scrap Book*
	Last Scrap Book
Jack London	*The People of the Abyss*
Arnold Bennett	
[Charles] Baudelaire	

[George Orwell]	*Burmese Days* *Down and Out in Paris and London*
John Galsworthy	*The Man of Property* *Justice* *The Silver Spoon*
'Beachcomber'	
[David Low]	*Colonel Blimp*
Alec Brown, Philip Henderson	[See below]
D. H. Lawrence	*Lady Chatterley's Lover*
Ronald Knox, Arnold Lunn, [G. K.] Chesterton	
[George Bernard] Shaw	*Major Barbara* *Captain Brassbound's Conversion* *Misalliance*
W. W. Jacobs	
Henri Barbusse, [Marcel] Proust, [André] Gide	
[Dmitri] Mirsky	*Intelligentsia of Great Britain*
[Joseph] Conrad	
W. H. Auden	
Upton Sinclair, William Morris, Waldo Frank	
Mr. N. A. Holdaway	
Karel Čapek (play)	*R.U.R.*
Jonathan Swift	*Gulliver's Travels.*
[Charles] Dickens	*Hard Times*
Mr. John Beevers	*World Without Faith*
H. G. Wells	*Men Like Gods* *The Dream* *The Sleeper Awakes* *Stories of Space and Time*
Aldous Huxley	*Brave New World*
Mr John Strachey	*The Coming Struggle for Power*
[Ezra] Pound, Wyndham Lewis, Roy Campbell,	
T. S. Eliot	
[Major] Douglas Credit group	
[Karl] Marx	*Capital*
[William] Shakespeare	

ARTICLE

L. J. HURST

Mr Alec Brown	*The Fate of the Middle Classes*
[Periodicals mentioned]	*New Statesman* *Punch* *Daily Worker* *Daily Mail* *Saturday Review* *News Chronicle*
[Mock Title] Comrade X	*Marxism For Infants*

- A version of this article was first published on the website of The Orwell Society on 22 April 2022. See https://orwellsociety.com/the-road-to-wigan-pier-references/.

NOTES

[1] 'The 7th volume in the series 'The Modern World: A Survey of Historical Forces', edited by H. A. L. Fisher. The author is given variously as William Ralph Inge and Dean Inge. First published by Ernest Benn in 1926, it is reprinted in same year and again in 1933. Published by Hodder and Stoughton in 1938. In 1953, Ernest Benn published a revised version with an extensive new preface. Published in New York by Charles Scribner's Sons, in 1926. A revised edition is published by McGraw-Hill in January 1953. It appears in a German translation in 1939 as *England: Inhalt: Das Land und seine Bewohner - Die Seele Englands - Das Weltreich - Industrialismus - Demokratie - Schlußbetrachtung* (translator: *Ins Deutsche übertragen durch Fritz von Bothmer*)

[2] First published by Reeves and Turner, in 1886, and re-issued by T. Fisher Unwin, in 1902. Translated from the French by Eleanor Marx Aveling.

NOTE ON THE CONTRIBUTOR

L. J. Hurst is a trustee of The Orwell Society with responsibility for research and digital presence. For the last ten years he has been a bookseller. He has published reviews and criticism on Orwell and others for most of his adult life and continues to contribute to the British Science Fiction Association and the Shotsmag.co.uk website.

Reflections on 'St Andrew's Day, 1935'

Douglas Kerr takes a close look at Orwell's fascinating poem and the structural and thematic part it plays in the novel *Keep the Aspidistra Flying*.

> Sharply the menacing wind sweeps over
> The bending poplars, newly bare,
> And the dark ribbons of the chimneys
> Veer downward; flicked by whips of air,
>
> Torn posters flutter; coldly sound
> The boom of trams and the rattle of hooves,
> And the clerks who hurry to the station
> Look, shuddering, over the eastern rooves,
>
> Thinking, each one, 'Here comes the winter!
> Please God I keep my job this year!'
> And bleakly, as the cold strikes through
> Their entrails like an icy spear,
>
> They think of rent, rates, season tickets,
> Insurance, coal, the skivvy's wages,
> Boots, school-bills, and the next instalment
> Upon the two twin beds from Drage's.
>
> For if in careless summer days
> In groves of Ashtaroth we whored,
> Repentant now, when winds blow cold,
> We kneel before our rightful lord;
>
> The lord of all, the money-god,
> Who rules us blood and hand and brain,
> Who gives the roof that stops the wind,
> And, giving, takes away again;
>
> Who spies with jealous, watchful care,
> Our thoughts, our dreams, our secret ways,
> Who picks our words and cuts our clothes,
> And maps the pattern of our days;

DOUGLAS
KERR

> Who chills our anger, curbs our hope,
> And buys our lives and pays with toys,
> Who claims as tribute broken faith,
> Accepted insults, muted joys;
>
> Who binds with chains the poet's wit,
> The navvy's strength, the soldier's pride,
> And lays the sleek, estranging shield
> Between the lover and his bride.

Dione Venables's excellent edition of *The Complete Poetry* (Finlay Publisher, 2015) allowed readers for the first time to review all of George Orwell's surviving work in verse. Orwell was a master of prose. The poetry is a secondary production, but he took his verse-writing seriously, published some of it, and it is an important part of his identity as an artist. This essay examines one of his better-known poems, 'St Andrew's Day', a fascinating piece in itself, but also in the structural and thematic part that it plays in the novel *Keep the Aspidistra Flying* (1936).

The poem was published in November 1935 in *The Adelphi*, a literary journal founded by John Middleton Murry and edited at this time by Orwell's friend Richard Rees (see *CWGO* X: 402-403). Its second appearance, untitled, was in the pages of *Keep the Aspidistra Flying*, where it is being composed by the hero (or anti-hero) of that novel, Gordon Comstock, the moth-eaten poet.

With its specific setting and imagery, 'St Andrew's Day' is a modern poem about modernity. Indeed, we could call it modernist, since in a number of ways it pays homage to the masters of the generation before Orwell's and Comstock's, the generation of T. S. Eliot, Ezra Pound, Virginia Woolf and James Joyce. The cultivated readers of *The Adelphi* would have been familiar with these writers, and would most likely have spotted that this author was placing himself in their company through the intertextuality of his poem – that is, the way his work refers to or incorporates elements of earlier writing.

THE PRECEDENT OF THE MODERNISTS

In particular, in its bleak urban landscape, with its scurrying commuters beset by anxieties and with nothing to believe in except the insufficient rewards of materialism, they would no doubt have detected the precedent of T. S. Eliot's London poem *The Waste Land*, of 1922 ('Unreal city,/Under the brown fog of a winter dawn…'). This had quickly established itself with the younger generation as the great iconic poem of the modern scene, especially as it was greeted with incomprehension and disgust by readers of more conservative tastes. You may remember a scene in *Brideshead Revisited* (1945), by Orwell's contemporary Evelyn Waugh, where the young aesthete Anthony Blanche recites Eliot's poem through a megaphone from a balcony in an Oxford college, to annoy his more hearty fellow students on their way to rowing practice.

Though 'St Andrew's Day' was published before the novel, we know from a letter to Brenda Salkeld (*CWGO* X: 369) that Orwell wrote it with the intention of including it in *Keep the Aspidistra Flying*. Dione Venables explains its place in the book:

> The book hosts a poem that evolved slowly throughout 168 of its 277 pages, beginning with one shy little two-line couplet on page 5, and then growing verse by verse in every chapter, finally emerging in its entirety on pages 167-168. This is a unique and fascinating way to present a poem, involving the reader at every point of its evolution (p. 35).

It is, indeed, fascinating, but it is not unique. The long final section in James Joyce's novel *A Portrait of the Artist as a Young Man* (1916) shows the hero, Stephen Dedalus, composing a poem, a villanelle, in just this way. Orwell was an admirer of Joyce, and in the Trafalgar Square scene in *A Clergyman's Daughter* (1935) he had already tried, with partial success, to imitate the dramatic-surrealistic modernism of the Nighttown section (chapter 15) of Joyce's novel *Ulysses* (1922). So this was another way in which Orwell was enrolling his own novel in the company of the great modernists: Joyce's portrait of the alienated poet in modernity from *A Portrait of the Artist*, and Eliot's fashionable (not insincere) pessimism about the bleakness and sterility of the modern world from *The Waste Land*, the adopted anthem of Orwell's generation.

This is not the whole story the poem has to tell about the kind of writer Orwell wanted to be. In his great essay 'Inside the Whale' (1940), Orwell was to sketch the literary history of his own lifetime. While he shows his admiration for the modernist writing of the 1920s, he says that its authors showed no interest in politics and contemporary events, but were entirely occupied with formal experimentation and questions of the aesthetic. Not everyone today would agree with this judgement, but it was widely held, as you can see in the critical writings of Stephen Spender and Louis MacNeice for example. With the 1930s, and the long political crisis from the rise of Hitler to the outbreak of war in 1939 (when Orwell was in the middle of writing 'Inside the whale'), a new generation of writers appeared, clustered round the charismatic figure of W. H. Auden, which was very much interested in politics and overwhelmingly leftist in conviction. These writers were less interested in aesthetic form than in political content, their work responding to the urgent issues of the day: unemployment, depression, the rise of fascism, the Spanish War, the Popular Front.

As 'St Andrew's Day' progresses, it begins to sound more like the work of this later generation – Orwell's own contemporaries – in its engagement with social-economic issues, developing into a political critique of capitalism and the consumer society. It now sounds less like Eliot and more like Auden. It moves outwards, as the novel does, from the small world of Gordon Comstock (the bending poplars, the torn poster and the trams are observed by Gordon in chapter 1 from the window of the bookstore where he works), to the critical, quasi-mythic vision of the tyranny of the Money-God, its power over everyone's lives.

This vision is expressed in verse and in prose: in the second half of the poem, and in the account (in chapter 7) of Gordon Comstock's thoughts in the moment when, as he walks the streets of London, the ending for his poem comes to him.

> Something deep below made the stone street shiver. The tube-train, sliding through middle earth. He had a vision of London, of the western world; he saw a thousand million slaves toiling and grovelling about the throne of money. The earth is ploughed, ships sail, miners sweat in dripping tunnels underground, clerks hurry for the eight-fifteen with the fear of the boss eating at their vitals. And even in bed with their wives they tremble and obey. Obey whom? The money-priesthood, the pink-faced masters of the world. The Upper Crust. A welter of sleek young rabbits in thousand guinea motor cars, of golfing stockbrokers and cosmopolitan financiers, of Chancery lawyers and fashionable Nancy boys, of bankers, newspaper peers, novelists of all four sexes, American pugilists, lady aviators, film stars, bishops, titled poets, and Chicago gorillas. When he had gone another fifty yards the rhyme for the final stanza of his poem occurred to him. He walked homeward, repeating the poem to himself....

ANTICIPATIONS OF *NINETEEN EIGHTY-FOUR*

It is a powerful (though still partly comic) vision of the world-wide empire of money, anticipating *Nineteen Eighty-Four*, though this tyranny is economic rather than authoritarian. *Keep the Aspidistra Flying* has more in common with *Nineteen Eighty-Four* than is sometimes realised. This prose passage and the poem are both reminders that the nightmare of Big Brother's regime is based on three things: Orwell's observation of totalitarian regimes in the 1930s and 1940s, his experience of imperial rule in Burma, and his socialist critique of capitalism.

Let me now go through 'St Andrew's Day' and pick out a few points of interest.

It's written in four-line stanzas, on a loose iambic and octosyllabic base (Who chílls our ánger, cúrbs our hópe) and with a single rhyme in each stanza, at the end of the second and fourth line. This is a rather unambitious poetic form. Orwell's early poetic hero A. E. Housman used octosyllabic quatrains in *A Shropshire Lad*, but Housman usually gave himself the trouble of two rhymes per stanza. Still, Auden and his friends often made use of simple, popular forms, such as the ballad, because they were accessible and close to popular song, and so felt more democratic, or less 'elitist' as we might now say, than more elaborate structures like the stately villanelle composed by Joyce's Stephen Dedalus.

Gordon Comstock's poem is not given a title in the novel, though the action does open on St Andrew's Day. Peter Davison thought that the title might be 'an afterthought (possibly not Orwell's) and suggested by the issue [of *The Adelphi*] in which the poem appeared' (*CWGO* X: 403). It may well be an afterthought, but it is hard to believe that Richard Rees or anyone else would have conferred so specific a title on the poem without consulting the poet. It is, in any case, highly apposite. St Andrew's Day, 30 November, is the last day of autumn. In English poetry autumn is very much a romantic season, with its mood of plenitude and melancholy; we may think of that most romantic of poems, John Keats's ode 'To autumn' (1820). But in Orwell's poem, all that is coming to an end. Winter is coming. St Andrew's Day is the end of romantic autumn, the beginning of modern winter. (Could there be some resonance in the fact that St Andrew is the patron saint of Scotland, and Orwell's views on the Scots, at this stage of his career, were distinctly negative? There is nothing in the poem to suggest he had Scotland or the Scots in mind.)

The poem is carefully constructed. Its first two stanzas set the urban scene. This is London on a cold and windy day, its parks and its public transport, its commuting workers (like the ones in *The Waste Land*) hurrying to the station in crowds, and yet each absorbed in their own thoughts, their own world. They look to the east – a cardinal direction often associated in poetry with sunrise, renewal and hope – but coming from the east is the east wind, presaging a bleak winter. These people are clerks, office workers: this is not a poem about the labouring classes but the lower-middle class, who also suffered the insecurity of the Depression years, and other worries of modern life in what Auden would later call the 'Age of Anxiety'. And so the third and fourth stanzas plunge us into the inner world of these people, to the thoughts and feelings which separate them from their fellows, but which also bind them together: they are all afraid of the same things.

ARTICLE

DOUGLAS KERR

'Please God I keep my job this year!' Unemployment was people's great anxiety in the 1930s. These Londoners worry about rent, rates (revised upwards in 1934), and the recurrent expenses of a household budget, including paying the skivvy, an unskilled female servant. The 'twin beds from Drage's' is a well-chosen detail. Drage's was a widely-known retail emporium which helped to create a mass market for domestic furniture in the interwar years, its success based on a clever 'out-of-income' (hire purchase) scheme, referenced here, and – appropriately for *Keep the Aspidistra Flying* – sophisticated advertising campaigns. It was a fitting agent for the money-god.

The fifth stanza is the middle of this nine-stanza poem, and is also the hinge point, the tropic or turning-point, of the whole. From here, all the rest of the poem is a single sentence, introducing the money-god and characterising him with a string of adjectival phrases (who rules us, who spies, who claims, who binds, and so on). With the 'groves of Ashtaroth' – a pagan goddess – we enter into a mythic, cultic language, the world of gods. The past was for pleasure; but now the wind has changed, and we are in the power of the money-god, a baleful entity who has been the subject of Gordon Comstock's obsessive thoughts throughout the novel. I feel there is something here of Nietzsche's sense of the transition from the unbridled classical world into the Christian era of resentment, guilt and subjection, though I admit Orwell was not much of a Nietzschean.

There is no arguing. The money-god is a *god*, and 'we' accept him as our rightful lord. His rule over us is a kind of blasphemy, a travesty of the Christian God, and it is absolute. This god is a jealous one and can do what he likes: like the God of Job in the Bible, this lord giveth with one hand and taketh away with the other. The money-god is consumer capitalism – he 'buys our lives and pays with toys' – but he is also beginning to sound like Big Brother, spying on us, abolishing privacy, surveying not only our waking conscious actions but even our inner lives, 'Our thoughts, our dreams, our secret ways'. He anticipates perhaps what Shoshana Zuboff calls (in her 2019 study) the 'surveillance capitalism' of the twenty-first century, but also the world of Oceania where Winston Smith's neighbour Parsons is arrested for being disloyal in his sleep. The money-god rules over a modern world in which people's emotional and spiritual lives are deformed by the inescapable materialism and competition around them. It was a theme often explored by Orwell's own literary heroes like T. S. Eliot and D. H. Lawrence.

PUZZLES OF THE LAST STANZA

The last stanza has its puzzles. The 'sleek estranging shield' must be a reference to a condom, although it's not entirely clear why it's the money-god who sponsors this intervention. But the contraceptive image does pick up on the theme of sexual frustration that runs through poor Gordon Comstock's life. Infertility is also one of the motifs of *The Waste Land*, in which the Fisher King is wounded and his lands are barren. But it also chimes through *Keep the Aspidistra Flying*, in which Gordon is – until the final chapter – the last of the Comstocks, and his family gene-pool has dried up and is unable to generate either descendants or new narrative ('Nothing ever *happened* in the Comstock family').

The conclusion also activates another of the novel's main preoccupations when it speaks of how the money-god 'binds with chains the poet's wit'. The poet is, of course, Gordon himself. At the start of the story he has left a good job as a copywriter in the New Albion Advertising Agency, because he thinks of himself as an artist and is unwilling to compromise his artistic integrity. But it is hard to live without the New Albion salary. Should he go back to his earlier employer?

The whole novel stages a dialectic, or perhaps a quarrel, between two kinds of language. On one hand is poetry, an ideal language still marked with a kind of nobility, but of absolutely no interest to most people, and of no practical use ('For poetry makes nothing happen,' as Auden was to write a few years later). On the other hand is the language of commercial advertising, with a rhetoric of its own, entirely devoted to persuading people to spend money on things they did not know they wanted. For Gordon Comstock it is a depressing choice. Here is poetry.

> The octosyllables flicked to and fro. Click-click, click-click! The awful, mechanical emptiness of it appalled him. It was like some futile little machine ticking over. Rhyme to rhyme, click-click, click-click. Like the nodding of a clock-work doll. Poetry! The last futility.

And here is advertising:

> The New Albion was one of those publicity firms which have sprung up everywhere since the war – the fungi, as you might say, that sprout from a decaying capitalism. It was a smallish rising firm and took every class of publicity it could get. It designed a certain number of large-scale posters for oatmeal stout, self-raising flour, and so forth, but its main line was millinery and cosmetic advertisements in the women's illustrated papers, besides minor ads in twopenny weeklies, such as Whiterose Pills for Female Disorders, Your Horoscope Cast by Professor Raratongo, The Seven Secrets of Venus, New Hope for the Ruptured, The Truth about Bad Legs, Drink Habit conquered in Three Days, and Cyprolax Hair Lotion Banishes all Unpleasant Intruders.

ARTICLE

DOUGLAS KERR

AND WHO IS THE ACTUAL AUTHOR?

One final question: who is the author of 'St Andrew's Day'? The poem in Joyce's *A Portrait of the Artist* has two functions. It is a poem, and a rather beautiful one. But it is also a poem written by Stephen Dedalus who is the hero of the novel but, it must be admitted, a sometime foolish, immature, selfish, over-romantic egotist. His villanelle is a characterisation: this is the kind of poem such a young man might well write – a bit precious, otherworldly, rather show-off, already quite old-fashioned.

So what about 'St Andrew's Day'? Orwell published it over his own name in *The Adelphi*. He must have hoped that readers would like it on its own terms. But in the novel he attributes it to a poet who is something of a comic figure, the moth-eaten Gordon Comstock, author of a collection of verse called *Mice*, a petulant, spoiled, very minor poet who will give up writing poems in the last chapter. Gordon is sometimes exasperating and ridiculous. Is the same true of 'St Andrew's Day'? 'Poetry! The last futility.' Does the novel show that poetry is futile, in the face of its all-powerful rival, the language of the money-god?

As I conclude, let me call on W. H. Auden again. At the end of the 1930s, which he called a 'low, dishonest decade', Auden too seemed uncertain of his vocation as a poet. In a different city, in another dated poem, 'September 1st 1939', fearful of the coming winter of a second world war, he contemplated the streets. 'From the conservative dark/Into the ethical life/The dense commuters come…' In a time of crisis, what did the poet have to offer? Auden had a tentative answer:

> All I have is a voice
>
> To undo the folded lie….

Orwell had some unkind things to say about Auden, but I think he would have approved of this modest declaration. What about Gordon Comstock?

- This article is based on a 'George Talk', organised by The Orwell Society, given online on 8 May 2022 (see https://orwellsociety.com/about-the-society/george-talks/).

NOTE ON THE CONTRIBUTOR

Douglas Kerr is the author of *Orwell and Empire* (Oxford University Press, 2022) and of *Wilfred Owen's Voices* (Oxford University Press, 1993), *George Orwell* (Northcote House Publishers, 2003*)*, *Eastern Figures* (Hong Kong University Press, 2008*)* and *Conan Doyle: Writing, Profession and Practice* (Oxford University Press, 2013). He was Professor of English and Dean of Arts at Hong Kong University, and is Honorary Research Fellow at Birkbeck College, London University.

ARTICLE

Why He Joined the I. L. P.: Orwell, Brockway and the Struggle for Socialism

John Newsinger examines the extraordinary (though shamefully neglected) life of Fenner Brockway and the importance of his socialist ideas and activism to an understanding of George Orwell's politics.

On 24 June 1938, the *New Leader* newspaper published an article, 'Why I join the I. L. P', written by George Orwell. He had been on the fringes of the Independent Labour Party for some time, but it was his experiences during the Spanish Civil War, both positive and negative, that had finally convinced him to take out a membership card on 13 June. In his article, he stresses that no thinking person 'could live in such a society as our own without wanting to change it' and he referenced both what he had seen of the empire in Burma and what he had seen of the impact of poverty and unemployment at home. Now, however, the situation was becoming desperate because fascism was on the rise. As a writer he had to throw himself into the struggle for socialism because 'the era of free speech is closing down'.[1] Of course, the freedom of the press in Britain had always 'been something of a fake, because in the last resort money controls opinion', but there had still been spaces in which dissident writers could operate. These spaces were inevitably going to be closed down whether it was next year, in ten years' time or even in twenty years, but it was coming. The only way to prevent this was to become involved in the socialist struggle and that meant joining the I. L. P. He had 'not lost all faith in the Labour Party', and still hoped for the election of a Labour government with 'a clear majority', even though 'we know what the history of the Labour Party has been'. Indeed, he confidently expected them 'to fling every principle overboard in order to prepare for an Imperialist war'. A political party was urgently needed, then, which, 'even in the face of persecution', would not compromise its socialist principles. The I. L. P's political stand had, as far as he was concerned, been vindicated by what he had seen in Spain and by how the I. L. P. had stood by its comrades in the P. O. U. M (the Partido Obrero de Unificación Marxista) despite a tidal wave of lies and slander. It would be steadfast in its socialist commitment even in the face of persecution and so he had taken the decision to join (*CWGO* XI: 167-169).

For Orwell, this was a big decision. At around the same time, he offered to begin writing regularly for the *New Leader*, but the editor, Archibald Fenner Brockway, turned him down. He thought Orwell's writing would be too literary and not suitable for a working class newspaper intended to be sold and read on the factory shop floor (Wadhams 1984: 101). Many years later Brockway confessed to Bernard Crick that this was 'one of the two great mistakes of my life' and we can all share his regret (Crick 1992: 348).[2]

What were the politics of this organisation that Orwell, enthused by the Spanish revolution, appalled by the crimes of Stalinism and driven on by the growing threat of fascism and war, had decided to join? This was, it is worth noting, the only political party that he was to ever join. One useful way to come at this question is through an examination of the politics of the man who had turned down his journalistic contributions, Fenner Brockway. Such an examination shows that the I. L. P. was considerably further to the left than is often acknowledged in some accounts of Orwell; indeed, that Orwell was joining a party that actually proclaimed itself to be a 'Revolutionary Socialist' organisation.[3] This obviously raises the question of the extent to which Orwell himself embraced this political stance. First though, Fenner Brockway.

FENNER BROCKWAY: SHAMEFULLY NEGLECTED

Brockway is a shamefully neglected figure in the history of the British left, still awaiting a biographer.[4] He was politically active for more than seventy years, first joining the Marxist Social Democratic Federation in his late teens and then, after only three months, defecting to the Independent Labour Party in November 1907. He worked on the party's newspaper, the *Labour Leader*, and eventually in 1912 became its 'responsible editor'. Brockway was a determined opponent of militarism and imperialism and remained true to these beliefs even in 1914. He was totally opposed to the European war that Britain joined on 4 August and threw himself into the campaign against it. This came to involve considerable personal risk of violence at the hands of pro-war vigilantes: on one occasion Brockway was badly beaten by five men who were only deterred from throwing him into a canal by a passer-by scaring them away (Brockway 1942: 48). How serious the threat could be is brought home by Brockway's account of an anti-war meeting in Bradford where a protester came armed with a hand grenade to throw at the speakers (Ramsay MacDonald and Fred Jowett), but 'his friends persuaded him to go to a nearby hotel and there disarmed him' (Brockway 1946: 134).

Founder of the No Conscription Fellowship in November 1914, Brockway's anti-war stance inevitably brought him into conflict with the authorities. He was imprisoned for ten days in Pentonville at the end of July 1916 for refusing to pay a fine and while there saw Roger Casement awaiting execution for treason for his involvement in the 1916 Irish Rising. Brockway was released when, against his wishes, the fine was paid for him. His next clash with the authorities saw him court-martialled for refusing to be conscripted and to obey military orders, a stand which saw him condemned to spend three years in prison. Even while he was inside he continued agitating and propagandising. In Walton Gaol, Liverpool, he celebrated the news of the outbreak of revolution in Russia in the twice weekly *Walton Leader* that he produced on 'about forty toilet paper pages' and which 'included news items, cartoons, serious articles, humorous stories and correspondence'. This was circulated among the conscientious objector prisoners. Inevitably he led a revolt against prison conditions which saw an elected committee draw up new rules which were followed for ten days by the inmates before he was sent to another prison. Here he spent eight months in solitary confinement, the first month half-starved on a punishment diet that was only ended when he was hospitalised. He later remembered how inspired he had been by events in Russia, hoping that the revolution would spread to Britain with 'our prison doors being opened by comrade workers and soldiers'. News of the outbreak of revolution in Germany in November 1918, particularly 'the Socialist Revolution in Bavaria', promised great changes. All this was, he later admitted, somewhat over-optimistic (Brockway 1942: 98, 115).

He was not released until April 1919. One point worth making here is that Brockway's wartime stance shows that he was both extremely brave and very tough. He emerged from prison a determined life-long advocate of prison reform. His I. L. P. pamphlet, *Prisons as Crime Factories,* was published that same year. This was the first of many interventions in pursuit of this cause. Once again he threw himself into socialist politics, supporting Indian independence, opposing militarism and fighting on behalf of the trade union movement. He first stood for the Commons in 1922 and again in 1924, both times unsuccessfully. During the 1926 General Strike, he edited the northern edition of the T. U. C. newspaper, the *British Worker*. As far as the I. L. P. was concerned, the General Strike was, according to Brockway, 'a revolutionary struggle: the organised working class against a capitalist government'. His experience producing the paper had a tremendous impact upon him, convincing him that 'Socialism cannot be public ownership only; it must include workers' participation in management, the essence of industrial democracy'.

ARTICLE

JOHN NEWSINGER

Even when the T. U. C. surrendered and abandoned the miners to fight on alone for another six months, he still hoped that the workers would fight on regardless, that 'the end of the strike might be the beginning of the revolution'. But instead, those workers who had come out on strike in support of the miners soon returned to work, often facing victimisation, pay cuts and the de-recognition of their unions. In the aftermath, the I. L. P. threw itself into supporting the locked-out miners, 'collecting money, food and clothing' and running 'a scheme for miners' children to stay with sympathisers'. A similar scheme had been run during the Dublin lock-out of 1913 when 20,000 workers went on strike. Many miners' children went to live with I. L. P. families while the lock-out continued and Brockway's own family had a Welsh boy, Raymond, from Pontypridd, stay with them for six months (Brockway 1977: 73-74). The defeat of the General Strike and of the miners led to widespread demoralisation throughout the labour movement, but the I. L. P. continued to try to pull the Labour Party to the left. As for Brockway, he again took over as editor of the I. L. P. newspaper, now the *New Leader*, was heavily involved with War Resisters' International and even briefly with the communist initiated League Against Imperialism.[5] In May 1929, he was elected to the Commons representing Leyton East and the Labour Party formed a government under Ramsay MacDonald.

IMPACT OF LABOUR GOVERNMENT'S FAILURE ON BROCKWAY
The failure of the 1929-1931 Labour government marked a crucial moment in Brockway's political trajectory. The I. L. P. came into conflict with the government over its failure to assist the increasing number of people losing their jobs as the Great Depression swept over the country and then its determination to cut benefits and wages at the insistence of the bankers. It was also critical of its use of large-scale repression against the Indian nationalist movement, something that Brockway was particularly concerned about. Indeed, he was to be suspended from the Commons in July 1930 for protesting against mass arrests. As he later recalled, the Labour government had responded to Gandhi's civil disobedience campaign with repression so that 'within six months sixty thousand Indians were imprisoned. I was shocked that a Labour Government should besmirch the record of the British working class in this way' (Brockway 1942: 204-205). In his outstanding biography of the celebrated Christian socialist, Fred Jowett, *Socialism Over Sixty Years*, published in 1946, the chapter chronicling the downfall of this government is suitably titled 'Socialism is betrayed'. He lost his Commons seat in the Labour rout in the 1931 general election.

How did he look back on his three years as an MP? He was to later compare these three years in the Commons with his three years in prison, remarking that 'I saw character deteriorate in Parliament more than in prison'. Drink was certainly one factor and he makes the point that some MPs went about their parliamentary business clearly inebriated without anything being said. He remembered one Labour minister actually 'winding up a debate on unemployment' and only able 'to stand with difficulty ... a workman would be sacked if he were found drunk at his bench'. He walked out in disgust. This was, of course, many years before Boris Johnson! Worse than that, though, was the way that parliament 'tended to blunt a keen sense of class struggle'. The fact was that the Commons was 'a club ... very often one saw Labour MPs falling to the glamour of the social life of the other side, steadily leaving their own class behind them'. Even so, he still found it hard to come to terms with the way, during this Labour government, Labour MPs who 'had been leading figures in their localities in the struggle of the working class were so docile and servile in the acceptance of the policy imposed on them by the Government'. When John Beckett stormed out of the Commons in 1930 taking the ceremonial mace with him in protest against the curbing of debate, Brockway was appalled at the response of most Labour MPs. Their outrage at his actions was 'a revelation of how deeply they had fallen in idolatry to the institutions of the capitalist State. They regarded Beckett's action as sacrilege' (Brockway 1942: 205-206, 222-223).

Not only did the Labour government attack the unemployed on behalf of the bankers, but the Prime Minister and his closest allies defected to the Tories when the scale of the cuts demanded proved too great for the T. U. C. to stomach. One of the consequences of the failure of this government was the I. L. P.'s decision, in July 1932, to disaffiliate from the Labour Party. Brockway was very much involved in this breakaway in his capacity as party chairman. They hoped, as Philip Williamson put it, to replace the Communist Party 'as the revolutionary vanguard' and broke with the Labour Party 'to the strains of "The Internationale"' (Williamson 1992: 467).

THE RISE OF FASCISM

Brockway was always very much an internationalist and, as the 1930s unfolded, developments abroad had a tremendous impact both on him and on the politics of the I. L. P. The rise of fascism, in particular, served to pull him even further to the left. He often spoke at socialist events across Europe. In 1931, he visited Poland and spoke at a 'huge joint demonstration of the Bund and the Polish I. L. P.'. It was violently attacked by the communists, then in the grip of the ferociously sectarian 'Third Period', and he was subsequently arrested by military police. The Comintern's 'Third Period' strategy was, of course, an important factor in Hitler's rise to power. On a number of occasions he visited Germany. In 1932, he did a speaking tour in Germany, 'the last British Socialist to do so before Hitler triumphed'. Meetings were attacked by the Brownshirts while Red Guards 'accompanied me whenever I was in the streets'. In Breslau, he spoke at the graveside of Ferdinand Lassalle (1825-1864), the jurist, activist and one of the founders of social democracy in Germany. He remembered the leader of the local socialist movement, Eckstein, who was to be 'one of the first victims of the Nazi terror, exhibited on a lorry as a Jew, imprisoned and dead within a week'. The I. L. P. established the 'Eckstein Fund' to assist the underground socialist resistance. He went on to speak in Leipzig where the Brownshirts mounted the most violent attack of his tour and, although they were beaten back, he feared that the Nazis were on the road to power. Hitler became Chancellor the following year and proceeded to destroy the German socialist and communist movements. Brockway's experiences in Germany had a profound impact on him. They convinced him that a parliamentary road to socialism was not tenable because 'in a decisive crisis reaction would suppress Parliament. I began to see that in the last resort the workers would have to depend on their strength in a direct struggle with the capitalist class. … Socialists were living in a fool's paradise if they thought that a majority in Parliament was enough'. Events in Spain were, Brockway concluded, to demonstrate dramatically the truth of this proposition (Brockway 1977: 111; Brockway 1942: 240, 278).

As for the threat of fascism in Britain, the I. L. P. was to play an important part in opposing Oswald Mosley's British Union of Fascists, including the massive protest against their attempt to march through London's East End on 4 October 1936, the celebrated Battle of Cable Street. Both the I. L. P. and the Communist Party claimed credit for organising the anti-fascist protest on this occasion, and it certainly seems as if it was the I. L. P. that actually took the initiative. But for many years afterwards the communists succeeded in effectively suppressing the I. L. P.'s role, claiming the battle for themselves. Brockway was there on the streets and was himself knocked to the ground (Brockway 1942: 272).

Brockway put down the I. L. P.'s failure to supplant the Communist Party as the dominant force on the left outside the Labour Party to the subsidy the communists received from the Soviet Union. The C. P., in 1937, had a membership of 'about 10,000' while the I. L. P. had 'a similar membership'. That was where the similarity ended. Whereas the I. L. P. had 'only a skeleton staff at Head Office, one weekly newspaper, one monthly journal, and three paid organizers', the C. P. 'has paid organizers in most of the large centres of Britain … has a daily newspaper (on which the loss must be very heavy), an elaborate monthly journal, and officials in a dozen subsidiary organizations'. It was, he thought, 'subsidised by the Communist International to the extent of thousands of pounds a year'. And this, of course, was why the C. P. leadership was prepared to subordinate itself to the Soviet Union, supporting the Moscow trials and throwing Marxism overboard in favour of the Popular Front. He was convinced that the 'betrayals … of the last three years' would have caused 'doubt and dismay' among ordinary C. P. members, many of whom were 'genuine Revolutionary Socialists' (Brockway 1938: 189-191).

HUNGRY ENGLAND

Brockway was not just concerned with the threat posed by fascism – never separating it from the fight against capitalism. It was the poverty, exploitation and misery it brought with it that had to be overthrown; indeed, it was capitalism that bred fascism. In 1932, Victor Gollancz published Brockway's *Hungry England*, a precursor of Orwell's *The Road to Wigan Pier*. The book is a powerful first-hand account of the appalling living conditions experienced by working class families across Britain (despite the book's title, he visited both Scotland and Wales). He wrote about his visit to Bilston in the West Midlands:

> I get the impression of a district devastated by war. There are large waste stretches pocked with holes and ridges just as though they had suffered a heavy bombardment. … There are houses in ruins with bricks scattered in confusion. There are houses with cracked walls and roofs, only prevented from falling down by wooden beams propped against them. … Surely no place could have grown up as ugly as this without some evil mind having deliberately planned to wipe out every trace of beauty. … I go down black streets with dusty cinder paths. The houses look as though they have inches of soot on them (Brockway 1932: 41-42).[6]

Bilston, Brockway tells his readers, was 'the birthplace of the British steel industry', but now most of the steel-works are closed and the town is in the grip of the most terrible poverty: 'The people are in old, drab clothes. The children are in torn clothes. They sit playing on the edge of the road or in groups on cinder patches.' He goes on: 'I find it difficult to describe the first house I visit. It would be more suitable for chickens than human beings. The walls and roof are cracked. … The wallpaper is peeling off in big patches, as in a disused house. The bricks are falling out …. a dirty brown stain streaks the wall, where the rain has come through … there are no carpets or linoleum on the floors.' The family living here exists on the edge of starvation with their rent of 6s 9d and fuel cost of 3s leaving them with some 19s of their means-tested benefit to live on. They tell him: 'It's not much more than starvation all the time.' Brockway records his horror at the conditions this family was existing under whereupon his guide told him: 'Come next door and you will see worse.' He confesses that he could not bear to (Brockway 1932: 46-47).[7]

In his account of his train journey up to Glasgow, he tells his readers of how he read in the newspaper of 'the suicide of an unemployed man, after he had killed his wife and child'. This was nothing new though. After the means test had been introduced in November 1931, he had begun to keep a record of the suicides that were a product of unemployment and poverty: 'There are twenty-nine of them' so far. He chronicled the misery that drove George Cree, Henry Fuller, Walter Milner, Thomas Cast, Walter Harris, James Cartland, Christopher Saunders, Seward Plummer, John Emptage, Percy Wright, Arthur Taylor, Thomas Sherratt and others to kill themselves. Working class men ground down, broken, by unemployment, poverty and the means test. This all makes for extremely grim reading. The account of poverty in Glasgow that follows is just as devastating (Brockway 1932: 170-179).

Altogether, the book is a tremendously powerful and moving account of the impact of capitalist crisis upon millions of working class men, women and children. For Brockway it was never just a matter of statistics and figures, but very much all about the misery, hardship and suffering inflicted on families and individuals. *Hungry England* deserves to be better known. Whether or not Orwell read it we do not know.

The following year, 1933, he published, again with Gollancz, a powerful, 288-page indictment of the international arms trade, *The Bloody Traffic*. This ended with a remarkable summoning up of the memory of the 'Hands Off Russia' movement and of the threatened General Strike that had ended British intervention against Soviet Russia in 1920. The British working class had declared that 'if war were declared against Russia, not a train should run, not a wheel in an engineering shed should turn, no coal should be dug – industry would stop dead'. In the event, the Lloyd George government backed down, but Brockway made clear his hope that any future similar confrontation would see 'the end, not only of a particular war, but the economic system from which wars come' (Brockway 1933: 287-288).

IN THE UNITED STATES

Brockway visited the United States soon after Franklin Roosevelt was installed as President and began introducing his New Deal. He published an account of his visit, *Will Roosevelt Succeed?: A Study of Fascist Tendencies in America*, in 1934. Looking back on the visit in his 1942 memoir, *Inside the Left*, he criticised the New Deal for not tackling 'the fundamental causes of capitalist crisis' and for 'being in many respects grotesque', but even so it compared favourably with 'the incompetent futility of the Labour Government in Britain'. What was most important about the New Deal, however, 'was the stimulus that it gave to Trade Union organisation and action'. He 'took part in strikes of textile workers in Paterson, New Jersey and of engineers in Detroit'. As he points out, the strike in Paterson was actually against a wage cut being imposed under New Deal legislation. In Detroit, the strike leader was 'an ex-Scottish ILPer'. Brockway spoke at a mass meeting where he was applauded and cheered by the strikers so enthusiastically that he was called back by the chairman to speak again. As he puts it, 'the class solidarity engendered by a strike leaps over all prejudices whether national or political' (Brockway 1942: 229, 232-233).

Among the American socialists he met during his visit, he was particularly impressed by the former Communist Party leader, Jay Lovestone. Having expelled the Trotskyists from the Communist Party in the U. S. A., Lovestone and his supporters were themselves expelled, despite being in a majority, for aligning themselves with Nikolai Bukharin in the struggle for power in the Soviet Union and opposing the 'Third Period' turn. He became a leading figure in the Bukharinite International Communist Opposition, one of whose strongest groups was the Spanish Bloque Obrero y Campesino (B. O. C.), led by Joaquim Maurin. In 1935, the B. O. C. was one of the organisations that came together to form the Partido Obrero de Unificación Marxista, better known as the P. O. U. M. Maurin was to make a powerful impression on Brockway and he describes hearing him speak just weeks before the military coup in Spain: '… whenever Maurin spoke his power was evident. … His description of the situation in Spain was one of the most masterly analyses I have ever heard. Less than six weeks later the storm which he saw coming broke.' Maurin was known, according to Brockway, as 'the Lenin of Catalonia' (Brockway 1942: 289).

On the return trip from America, he describes how a troupe of Paramount dancing girls, travelling tourist class, were asked to put a performance on for the first class passengers. Tourist and third class passengers would be allowed to attend but only if they wore evening dress. The troupe refused unless the dress qualification was dropped. It was 'and that night the tourist and third class invaded the first class quarters en masse' (Brockway 1942: 236). This episode inspired Brockway's only novel, *Purple Plague: A Tale of Love and Revolution*, published in 1935. In the novel, a transatlantic liner is infected by a deadly virus, is refused entry to any ports and neither passengers nor crew are allowed to disembark. Eventually the crew and the third class passengers rebel, overthrow the officers and eliminate the privileges of the first class. The ship-board revolution establishes a democratic classless society, setting an example for the world.[8]

BROCKWAY, ORWELL AND SPAIN

Brockway wrote four volumes of autobiography and it is interesting to see how Orwell figures in the succeeding volumes. In his 1942 *Inside the Left*, Orwell hardly appears at all. John McNair is celebrated as the I. L. P.'s man in Spain, the hero of the hour. Indeed, Ethel Mannin's contribution to the struggle gets considerably more attention than Orwell's.[9] This had changed by his 1963 volume, *Outside the Right* and his 1977 volume, *Towards Tomorrow*, and by his 1986 volume, *98 Not Out*, he was crediting Orwell's 'warning of authoritarianism' with his decision to 'call myself a libertarian Socialist' (Brockway 1986: 3). Clearly, as Orwell became more important and influential a figure so the significance of his earlier role was reassessed, and not just by Brockway it must be said. In *Inside the Left*, it is 'Eric Blair, (George Orwell, the author)' who is mentioned in passing as having escaped from the communists, crossing the frontier into France together with the much more important John McNair and with Stafford Cottman, 'a boy of eighteen with the heat of a giant' (Brockway 1942: 303).

This is, then, an interesting testimony to how little impact *Homage to Catalonia* had at the time of its publication in 1937. Shunned by most of the left, two years later at the start of the Second World War, it had sold only 900 copies. By the time of *Outside the Right*, Brockway is celebrating his 'companionship' with Orwell and remembered how he 'came to our I. L. P. summer schools and won our affection and admiration by the gentleness of his character and the integrity of his mind. I remember walking one evening with him up and down a narrow lane … whilst almost shyly he expressed his desire to devote his writing to a libertarian form of Socialism'. Orwell, he reminds his readers, was shot in the throat in Spain. He goes on: 'When later I read his *Animal Farm* and *1984*, I thanked all the gods that the fascist bullet had not sped a quarter inch to the right' (Brockway 1963: 25). And in *Towards Tomorrow*, he wrote of how he had met Eric Blair at the I. L. P. head office where they had discussed his 'going to Spain'. Brockway comments that Orwell was 'attracted by the libertarian Socialism of the I. L. P. but had been disillusioned by visits to London branches where Communists and Trotskyists had wrangled'. Here, it was not Orwell who made Brockway a libertarian socialist, but rather the I. L. P.'s libertarian socialism that impressed Orwell (Brockway 1977: 120).

Clearly Orwell's importance at the time of the Spanish revolution was magnified over the years as his posthumous influence increased. But what about the influence that Brockway and the I. L. P. had on Orwell? Certainly the evidence suggests that Orwell was influenced by the I. L. P. before he went to fight in Spain but that he was at the same time put off by not just the sectarian wrangling he saw in the London branches, but also by the crankishness, as far as he was concerned, of many of its middle class members, which he famously denounced in *The Road to Wigan Pier*. Indeed, when he was about to go to fight in Spain, he had still not decided whether he would join with the Communist International Brigades or with the I. L. P. contingent fighting with the P. O. U. M., and he was actually preparing to transfer to the International Brigades just before the May 1937 rising in Barcelona.

By the time he came back from Spain any reservations he may have had about the I. L. P. had obviously been put to rest. As for the communists, he no longer regarded them as being in the socialist camp at all. As we have seen, he joined the I. L. P. on 13 June 1938, at a time moreover when it was being bitterly attacked by the Communist Party for either being in league with the fascists or for actually being a Trotskyist-fascist organisation. What were the I. L. P.'s politics at this time? Two publications, both written by Brockway and that we know Orwell read, are useful in this regard: his pamphlet, *The Truth About Barcelona*, published by the I. L. P. in 1937, and his book, *Workers Front*, published by Secker & Warburg in 1938.

THE TRUTH ABOUT BARCELONA

In August 1937, Orwell published an article, 'Eye-witness in Barcelona', in the I. L. P. discussion journal, *Controversy*, edited by C. A. Smith. Here, he endorsed Brockway's *The Truth About Barcelona* as 'so far as my knowledge goes … entirely accurate' with his article merely adding 'a few footnotes upon several of the most-disputed points' (*CWGO* XI: 55). This article had previously been rejected by the *New Statesman* and, as he complained in a letter to his friend Rayner Heppenstall, it was impossible to get the truth about what had and was happening in Barcelona even 'mentioned in the English press, barring the publications of the I. L. P.'. He went on to tell Heppenstall that he was also having to change his publisher from Victor Gollancz as he was 'part of the Communist-racket' and had rejected his proposed book on Spain, *Barcelona Tragedy*, 'though not a word of it was written yet'. Knowing that Orwell had fought in the ranks of the P. O. U. M. was enough for him to be dropped (ibid: 53). The I. L. P. not only published the article but was also instrumental in getting *Barcelona Tragedy* or

Homage to Catalonia, as it was to become, published. Reg Reynolds and John Aplin, representing the I. L. P., had been in discussions with Fredric Warburg regarding the publication of a number of socialist books written from an I. L. P. perspective including Ethel Mannin's *Women and the Revolution*, Brockway's own *Workers Front*, Victor Serge's *From Lenin to Stalin* as well as Orwell's *Barcelona Tragedy*. According to Brockway, Warburg was 'sympathetic to the I. L. P.' at this time (Brockway 1977: 120). Secker & Warburg were to publish a number of I. L. P.-sponsored books as well as those already mentioned, among them C. L. R. James's *World Revolution* and *Black Jacobins* and Reg Reynolds's *The White Sahibs in India*. Warburg was to continue to publish Orwell, including both *Animal Farm* and *Nineteen Eighty-Four*.

The Truth About Barcelona was a fifteen-page pamphlet that sold for one penny. In its pages, Brockway chronicled the revolutionary response to the fascist coup in Spain with a situation of dual power developing behind the Republican lines. On the one side there was the Popular Front government and on the other the workers' councils dominated by the anarchists and to a lesser extent the P. O. U. M. The situation was so grim that both the anarchists and the P. O. U.M. ('a considerable departure in its policy') agreed to join the government with the P. O. U. M. securing a promise that 'a programme for the socialisation of industry would be applied'.

For Brockway this was a mistake, helping restore 'the power of the capitalist State machine'. He wrote: 'At the time the danger was not fully recognised, though Marxist principles should have provided a warning. Marx taught that the workers' revolution will require new instruments of administration and that these instruments must be based, not on the structure of the Capitalist State, but on the organisations of the working class. What has subsequently happened in Barcelona proves how accurate was the analysis of the founder of scientific Socialist theory'. Instead of the revolution moving forward, the communists urged rolling it back and 'a return to a Democratic Capitalist Republic'. The P. O. U. M. was the main obstacle to this counter-revolution, doing its best to sustain 'the revolutionary spirit'. Its slogan was 'that the war and the revolution were indivisible'. It was routinely slandered and abused as a result, condemned as a Trotskyist organisation, which Brockway makes absolutely clear was not the case. Russian intervention was decisive however in strengthening the counter-revolution. The conflict came to a head in Barcelona in May 1937 and Brockway briefly chronicles the rising. As far as he was concerned, throughout this period, the P. O. U. M. followed 'the historical line of Marxist Socialists' and he wholeheartedly endorses their stance. Moreover, he insists that they have emerged stronger from the struggle so that, the position in Spain is more hopeful, not less hopeful, from the point of view of the Socialist Revolution'. This was sadly a serious misjudgement. He goes on to explain how communist policy in Spain was determined not by the class struggle, but by the Soviet Union's need for an alliance with 'the so-called "democratic" Capitalist nations against Germany'. This had produced a remarkable turnaround from events in Russia in 1917, so that, in Spain, the communists 'took the part of the Mensheviks' while the P. O. U. M. 'fulfilled the historic role the Bolsheviks fulfilled'. It was the communists who were putting down, crushing, a workers revolution! This communist betrayal meant that across Europe workers were turning to the likes of the P. O. U. M. and the I. L. P. He looked forward to the Spanish workers led by the P. O. U. M. winning a victory that 'will not only shatter Fascism, but lay the foundations of the new Workers' State of Socialism. It is our duty to speed the coming of that day' (Brockway 1937: 5-7, 11, 13, 14-15). Once again he was somewhat over-optimistic.

Brockway's hope that the P. O. U. M. would emerge stronger and that the revolution would roll forward was, of course, soon confronted with the reality of a communist triumph and the successful crushing of the revolutionary left in Spain. McNair, Orwell and Cottman having to flee the country is testimony to that. What is important for our purposes, though, is that Orwell endorsed this quite unequivocal celebration of socialist revolution in Spain and soon after joined the I. L. P. Even more telling in this respect is Brockway's *Workers Front*, published early in 1938.

WORKERS FRONT

Workers Front was a substantial political statement of where the I. L. P. stood in 1938. It was just over 250 pages long and dedicated to 'Jeanne and Joaquim Maurin'. The book opens with a chapter on the crisis of capitalism, which is followed by a chapter examining the weaknesses of the international working class in the face of this crisis. Brockway describes the British labour movement as 'probably more demoralised than any in the world', outside of Italy and Germany. While British workers were, he insisted, ready to fight on the shop floor, the union leaders stood in the way. That 'the spirit of class action' still lived on in Britain had been shown in February 1935, 'when the mass action of British workers compelled the National Government to withdraw its new Unemployment Regulations'. And he was convinced that if the National government had intervened on Franco's side and had 'bombarded Barcelona and Valencia' then the likelihood was that the 'class struggle would have become nakedly apparent in Britain as well'. A Revolutionary Socialist Party was needed that 'must base itself on the class struggle and that struggle

JOHN NEWSINGER

must aim at the overthrow of both the economic and political structure of the Capitalist State'. He was absolutely emphatic that the 'hope that Capitalism can be transformed to Socialism through the means of the Capitalist State – its Parliaments, civil service, armed forces, judiciary – is an illusion'. Instead, the capitalist class had to be defeated 'through Workers' Councils or Soviets … and in the last resort, if necessary, through their own workers' army … responsible to their Councils or Soviets'. He could not have been clearer. In 1938, the I. L. P. was advocating the carrying out of a 1917-style revolution in Britain with itself playing the role of the Bolsheviks. Certainly, the Communist Party could not play this role. It was completely subordinate to the Stalin regime and its policies were intended to advance the interests of Russian foreign policy rather than the interests of the British or any other working class. The dramatic abandonment of the ultra-sectarian 'Third Period' strategy in favour of the Popular Front strategy was astonishing: 'History has not shown a more complete volte face.' The 1939 Hitler-Stalin Pact was, of course, an even more dramatic volte face! From condemning the likes of the Labour Party as fascists, when they adopted the Popular Front strategy, the communists put on hold, indeed effectively abandoned, their revolutionary politics altogether, in order to ally with even 'the Liberal Capitalists' to fight fascism and to support an alliance between the Soviet Union and Britain and France. In effect, as far as the communists were concerned, the 'class struggle against Capitalism is to retire in favour of an all-class coalition for "democracy"'. For Brockway, the result was always going to be disaster and this had already been demonstrated in France where the Popular Front government had saved capitalism during the great wave of sit-in strikes during the summer of 1936. Now it was being even more clearly demonstrated by events in Spain (Brockway 1938: 24, 34, 35, 60, 72, 85).

He proceeds to chronicle events in Spain in much more detail than in his earlier pamphlet. Four chapters (75 pages) describe and analyse the struggle in Spain, beginning with 'The Popular Front in Spain', then 'Socialist Revolution or Capitalist Democracy?', next 'The Retreat from the Social Revolution' and ending with 'The Counter-Revolution'. In their suppression of the P. O. U. M. following the Barcelona rising, the communists were using 'the tactic of Hitler'. Forty members of the P. O. U. M. central council were arrested, some four hundred local officials, activists and foreign socialists assisting in the fighting were rounded up and the P. O. U. M. newspapers were suppressed. This 'coup d'etat against the P. O. U. M. was carried out by the Secret Service Police, of which the Communists had taken control, and which they organized on the model of the Russian O. G. P. U.'. Even if Franco were defeated, it was very unlikely that parliamentary democracy would be restored. More likely was some kind of 'Capitalist dictatorship'. Nevertheless, he ends on an optimistic note: 'One looks forward with absolute confidence to the coming of the day when the Spanish workers and peasants will rise in unity and strength, and learning from the mistakes of this tragic period, will be satisfied with nothing less than the social justice, equality and freedom which only the overthrow of Capitalism can bring' (Brockway 1938: 123, 145-146, 147, 148).

Brockway goes on to identify a number of international organisations that offer hope for the working class and for the struggle for socialism. There is the International Bureau for Revolutionary Socialist Unity (that the I. L. P. was affiliated to), the International Communist Opposition, the Anarchist International and the Trotskyist Fourth International.[10] He hoped for co-operation between these organisations, for some kind of 'Revolutionary Socialist unity', and thought that events in Spain might have made this possible. But what about the Labour Party? Its working class members and supporters were crucial and 'without their support Revolutionary Socialists cannot hope to achieve success', but the 'undemocratic structure of the Labour Party is the first obstacle to working class unity'. He considers the problems involved in affiliating with the Labour Party, noting the leadership's successful suppression of the Socialist League in 1937. The threat of expulsion led to the organisation disbanding in May of that year. Nothing had changed since the I. L. P. voted to disaffiliate. He made clear that as far as he was concerned 'the I. L. P. was correct in leaving the Labour Party in 1932', not least because since then 'the I. L. P. has now founded itself firmly on the basis of the class struggle'. And the quality of the membership had improved because it no longer attracted the 'political careerists' who saw it as a useful 'stepping-stone to Parliament and to office'. Affiliation was not a question of principle, however, but of tactics and he did not rule it out in the future. But the Labour Party would have to change and accept that the I. L. P. could oppose from the inside just about every Labour Party policy in 'a comradely spirit'. Rejoining the Labour Party would only be possible if the I. L. P. could retain 'its Revolutionary Socialist policy'; indeed, any weakening of its commitment to the class struggle 'would be a backward step rather than an advance'. He urged unity on the left, but not in the form of a class collaborationist Popular Front, but of 'a Revolutionary Workers' Front' (Brockway 1938: 204, 214-215, 217, 254). It is worth making the point that all through this period, the I. L. P. was losing members.

'FASCISM AND CAPITALISM ARE AT BOTTOM THE SAME THING'
How did Orwell respond to Brockway's *Workers Front*? He reviewed it on 17 February 1938 in the pages of the *New English Weekly*, that

JOHN NEWSINGER

is, before he took the decision to join the I. L. P. Here he focuses on Brockway's assault on the Popular Front which he comments 'is written from the standpoint that it is now usual to denounce as "Trotskyist"'. For Orwell, the Popular Front is just a 'polite name' for 'class collaboration' and Brockway was right to assert that its only result is 'fixing the capitalist class more firmly in the saddle'. At the moment the Popular Front is 'only an idea' in Britain, but 'it has already produced the nauseous spectacle of bishops, Communists, cocoa-magnates, publishers, duchesses and Labour MPs marching arm in arm to the tune of "Rule Britannia"'. Against this, Brockway argues that fascism can only be fought 'by attacking capitalism'. Orwell endorses this, but takes exception to Brockway's restricting the working class to manual labourers, insisting that 'there now exists a huge middle class whose interests are identical with those of the proletariat'. This middle class – the white collar workers of today – have to be won over to the socialist cause. To do this, the socialist movement 'should shed some of its nineteenth century phraseology'. This was not a new criticism, but one that Orwell had already put forward in *The Road to Wigan Pier*. One suspects that this was the reason Brockway turned down his offer to write for *New Leader*. Orwell ends the review acknowledging that the book is 'written from what is at the moment the most unpopular angle', but insists that its arguments 'ought not to be neglected even by those who are hostile to its main implications' (*CWGO* XI: 123-124). Four months later he joined the I. L. P.

AFTERWARDS

Orwell did not remain a member of the I. L. P. for long. He was to end his membership once the Second World War had begun, and he, at least in part in response to the Hitler-Stalin Pact, had embraced the politics of 'revolutionary patriotism'. In the early years of the conflict, he saw events very much through Spanish glasses and tried to adapt the politics of the P. O. U. M. and of the I. L. P. to the situation in war-time Britain in a way that he thought more appropriate than the position taken up by his former I. L. P. comrades. It is worth quoting from his article, 'Our opportunity', that appeared in *Left News* in January 1941. Here he defended revolutionary patriotism, arguing that England 'was on the road to revolution', that this was 'the same impulse that moved the Paris workers in 1793, the Communards in 1871, the Madrid trade unionists in 1936 – the impulse to defend one's country, and to make it a place worth living in' and that 'the feeling of all true patriots and all true Socialists is at bottom reducible to the

"Trotskyist" slogan: "The war and the revolution are inseparable"' (*CWGO*: XII: 345-346, 350).

Once he had concluded that there was not going to be a revolution and that the British capitalist class had been saved by the Soviet Union and the United States, he still remained committed to the politics he had publicly embraced when he joined the I. L. P. – at least as far as domestic politics were concerned. One crucial insight he remained true to up until his death was the belief that any serious attempt to abolish capitalism and end the wealth and power of the capitalist class would be forcibly resisted. This was a lesson from the 1930s he never forgot. Orwell was to collaborate with Brockway after the war in the Freedom Defence Committee following the arrest of anarchists and pacifists for encouraging soldiers to withdraw from the war effort; indeed, Brockway chaired one meeting at which Orwell spoke at Conway Hall in London on 7 November 1945.

What of Brockway? He remained one of the leaders of the I. L. P. throughout the war, but became increasingly disillusioned with what he came to regard as the futility and impotence of revolutionary politics. Indeed, he was to later make clear that the I. L. P.'s disaffiliation from the Labour Party had, in retrospect, been a terrible mistake, 'a stupid and disastrous error' (Brockway 1977: 107). He finally broke with the I. L. P. after the 1945 general election and a year later rejoined the Labour Party. He was actually offered a peerage, but refused: 'I wanted to abolish that undemocratic institution' (Brockway 1963: 43). He was elected to the Commons in 1950, a staunch 'Bevanite', and went on to help found War on Want, the Movement for Colonial Freedom and the Campaign for Nuclear Disarmament. He was a determined opponent of racism with the front of his London home being on one occasion painted over with swastikas and racist slogans courtesy of Colin Jordan's Nazis. After he lost his Commons seat in 1964, a victim of vicious racist campaigning, in the best traditions of British Labourism he became Baron Brockway, but he continued campaigning for another twenty odd years.

NOTES

[1] On questions of style, *George Orwell Studies* has socialism, communism, fascism etc but Communist Party etc. Where Orwell and Brockway use in their writings Socialism, Fascism, Capitalism etc the journal follows their style

[2] For a useful study of Brockway and the *New Leader* see Kent (2010)

[3] For the history of the I. L. P. in this period see Cohen (2007), Bullock (2017), Laybourn (2020) and Thwaites (2020)

[4] It is astonishing that Brockway still awaits a biographer. He was also the author of four volumes of autobiography and of numerous other books including

excellent biographies of Fred Jowett and the Labour movement activist and pacifist Alfred Salter (1949) and a history of the Levellers and the Diggers (1980)

[5] The League Against Imperialism, which Brockway briefly chaired, was established in February 1927 in Brussels with many delegates from the colonies in attendance, including from India, China, South Africa, Indonesia, the Philippines, Cuba, Haiti, Egypt, Indochina and Palestine. Jawaharlal Nehru was among the delegates from the colonies. Among the European delegates were Albert Einstein, Henri Barbusse, Ernst Toller along with George Lansbury, Ellen Wilkinson and, of course, Fenner Brockway

[6] For a useful discussion of *Hungry England* see Christopher Olewicz, 'Fenner Brockway and the return of hungry England'. Available online at independentlabour.org.uk

[7] ibid

[8] For a useful discussion see Christopher Olewicz, 'Brockway's book and the post-covid search for a utopian future'. Available online at independentlabour.org.uk

[9] McNair escaped from Spain, together with Orwell and Cottman, and went on to become general secretary of the I. L. P. in 1939, a post that he held until 1955. In his seventies, he did a degree at Durham University and for his MA wrote his thesis on George Orwell

[10] The International Bureau was established in 1932 and had affiliates in Norway, Bulgaria and Holland. After 1935, these were joined by affiliates from Palestine, Greece and Czechoslovakia along with the P. O. U. M. In 1939, the International Communist Opposition affiliated, bringing in a number of other organisations. Its headquarters were in London until 1939 and, according to Gidon Cohen, throughout these years, 'the I. L. P. was a prime mover in the Bureau' (see Cohen 2007: 70)

REFERENCES

Brockway, Archibald Fenner (1932) *Hungry England*, London: Victor Gollancz

Brockway, Archibald Fenner (1933) *The Bloody Traffic,* London: Victor Gollancz

Brockway, Archibald Fenner (1934) *Will Roosevelt Succeed? A Study of Fascist Tendencies in America,* London: George Routledge

Brockway, Archibald Fenner (1937) *The Truth About Barcelona*, London: Independent Labour Party

Brockway, Archibald Fenner (1938) *Workers Front,* London: Secker & Warburg

Brockway, Archibald Fenner, (1942) *Inside the Left: Thirty Years of Platform, Press, Prison and Parliament*, London: George Allen & Unwin

Brockway, Archibald Fenner (1946) *Socialism Over Sixty Years: The Life of Jowett of Bradford*, London: George Allen & Unwin

Brockway, Archibald Fenner (1963) *Outside the Right*, London: George Allen & Unwin

Brockway, Archibald Fenner (1977) *Towards Tomorrow*, St Albans: Hart-Davis, MacGibbon

Brockway, Archibald Fenner (1986) *98 Not Out,* London: Quartet Books

Bullock, Ian (2017) *Under Siege: The Independent Labour Party in Interwar Britain*, Edmonton: AU Press

Cohen, Gidon (2007) *The Failure of a Dream: The Independent Labour Party from Disaffiliation to World War 11*, London: I. B. Tauris

Crick, Bernard (1992) *George Orwell: A Life*, London: Penguin

Davison, Peter (ed.) (1998) *The Complete Works of George Orwell* (*CWGO*) XX volumes, London: Secker & Warburg

Kent, Hazel (2010) 'A paper not so much for the armchair but for the factory and the street': Fenner Brockway and the Independent Labour Party's *New Leader* 1926-1946, *Labour History Review,* Vol. 75, No. 2 pp 208-226

Laybourn, Keith (2020) *The Independent labour Party 1914-1939: The Political and Cultural History of a Socialist Party*, London: Routledge

Thwaites, Peter (2020) *Waiting for the Workers: A History of the Independent Labour Party 1938-1950*, Gloucester: The Choir Press

Wadhams, Stephen (1984) *Remembering Orwell*, London: Penguin

Williamson, Philip (1992) *National Crisis and National Government: British Politics, the Economy and Empire 1926-1932*, Cambridge: Cambridge University Press

NOTE ON THE CONTRIBUTOR

John Newsinger is a retired academic. He is the author of *Orwell's Politics* and of *Hope Lies in the Proles: George Orwell and the Left*. His most recent book is *Chosen by God: Donald Trump, the Christian Right and American Capitalism*. He has reviewed nearly forty books on the Trump Presidency.

ARTICLE

ARTICLE

Mary Poppins at the Ministry of Tweets

John Rodden examines the fate of the star-crossed Disinformation Governance Board, set up by the Biden administration in April 2022 and closed down within two months, having been lambasted and lacerated from all sides as an Orwellian 'Big Brother' operation.

ONCE UPON … A BRIGHT COLD DAY IN APRIL? A FAIRY STORY

Dear Reader, did you perhaps share my fantasy? A fantasy that, in the aftermath of the 2020 American election and Washington 'regime change', the relevance of the language and vision of *Nineteen Eighty-Four* might soon wane in 'the land of the free'? I, for one, briefly imagined exactly that, given that the Democratic Party would be controlling both the executive and legislative branches of the federal government.

And yet, recent events demonstrate – once again, as ever – that Orwell and *Nineteen Eighty-Four*, or rather, to use the American title, *1984*, are equal opportunity employers. How did I succumb to such utopian delusions – after Nixon's secret White House taping system with his 'expletives deleted' and Reagan's 'Peacekeeper missiles' and George W. Bush's W. M. D. fabrications? After Clinton's redefinitions of 'what "is" is' and Obama's 'Yes, we scan' snooping on foreign leaders?

Yes, as if on schedule, it turns out that some distinctive features of 'The Orwellian Amerika of Donald J. Trump' – as I titled an article in 2020 about the upcoming presidential election – possess their Bidenesque counterparts. Not surprisingly, the rich ironies characterising 'Orwellian Amerika' have re-emerged into the limelight in the run-up to another election – the 2022 mid-term races in November. What I had termed 'the Donald's Ministry of Alternative Facts' gave way in April 2022 to Biden's 'Disinformation Governance Board' (D. G. B.). Or rather, 'The Ministry of Tweets' headed by a Biden appointee popularly known as 'Mary Poppins'. Welcome to Amerika, 2022.

EXCERPTS FROM WINSTON'S DIARY, OR THE 'MUSKY' ORIGINS OF AMERIKA'S K. G. B. – OOPS, D. G. B.

It was a bright cold 27 April in Washington, Oceania – er, Amerika. The citizenry was transfixed by speculation that multi-multi billionaire Elon Musk, the founder and C.E.O. of Tesla and SpaceX, planned to purchase Twitter.

Meanwhile, routine congressional testimony was underway. Alejandro Mayorkas, secretary of the Department of Homeland Security, was asked about the agency's activities in response to a friendly question from a Democratic congresswoman. What was D. H. S. doing to combat 'disinformation' on technology platforms that targeted minority communities? Mayorkas replied that the department had just launched a 'new initiative' aimed at taking aggressive measures to deal with such issues, including Russian disinformation about Ukraine, lies fed by smugglers to migrants seeking to enter the U. S. illegally and 'other threats' to U. S. national security. Central to this new initiative was the formation of a Disinformation Governance Board which would 'monitor' internet activity and formulate policies to handle cases of disinformation.

Throughout the cybersphere, blogosphere and worlds of news and opinion alarms rang out about Newspeak, thought policing and impending trips to Room 101. It may not have represented 'a watershed moment in history', as the libertarian *Activist Post* fretted days later. Yet it was as if Oceania's clocks were suddenly striking thirteen – and, indeed, as if Amerikans' telescreens were about to get mandatory upgrades beyond 5G networks, courtesy of the Minipax functionaries – all aimed, of course, to 'make the world safe for democracy'. Or rather, autocracy.

THE SUPERCALIFRAGILISTICEXPIALIDOCIOUS SPEECH POLICE

As more information about the D. G. B. dribbled out, it was learned that Nina Jankowicz, a 33-year-old 'disinformation specialist', had been appointed its executive director. That announcement raised eyebrows – and Jankowicz immediately launched into a spirited Tiktok parody of Mary Poppins, garbing herself as the nanny of Amerikan speech and delivering a rousing adaptation of MP's 'supercalifragilisticexpialidocious' show stopper complete with satirical references to Rudy Giuliani, Covid skeptics, and 'hucksters … saying lies in Congress' (a.k.a. Republicans).

Jankowicz introduced herself to the Amerikan public with her immortal Twitter line: 'You can just call me the Mary Poppins of disinformation.' Thousands of observers would do just that during her short reign as Biden's so-called 'Disinformation Czarina' which, as it turned out, would last no more than a mere four weeks.

ARTICLE

JOHN RODDEN

It was hardly surprising that, within hours, the hashtag #MinistryofTruth was trending and that conservatives and libertarians were tweeting 'Big Brother Biden' and blaring that the D. G. B. was 'straight out of Orwell's *1984*'. Undeniably, the name 'Disinformation Governance Board' was something quite atrocious (perhaps predictably so, given that it was a unit in the Orwellian-sounding 'Homeland Security' department).

Critics charged that executive director Jankowicz was, certainly, a 'disinformation expert' since she had relentlessly promoted disinformation. She had repeatedly endorsed the allegedly phony Christopher Steele dossier used to investigate Donald Trump's 2020 campaign. She had dismissed *New York Post* reports during the 2020 election campaign about a laptop computer with compromising photographs and emails – purportedly owned by Biden's son, Hunter – as a Russian disinformation campaign, later adding that 'We should view it as a Trump campaign product.'

Already by 28 April, right-wing voices were fretting that we were 'now seeing the outlines of how the fourth branch of government are planning to keep control over information, specifically public discussion on Big Tech platforms' as a writer for *The Conservative Treehouse* wrote in an article headlined 'Deep state response, Department of Homeland Security will establish Disinformation Board with obvious agenda'. Conservative economist Greg Price, former president of the National Economic Association, tweeted: 'The government is so afraid of Elon Musk owning Twitter that they literally created a real-life Ministry of Truth less than a week after he bought it.' Some Democrats agreed. The political activist and former Democratic congressional candidate Dan Sanchez chimed in: 'Elon Musk buys Twitter to save free speech and days later President Biden announces a Ministry of Truth. It's like we're living through an Ayn Rand/George Orwell novel mash-up.'

They were echoed by an influential and respected libertarian voice, the constitutional law scholar Jonathan Turley. No stranger to controversy, especially since his derision of the 'politically motivated' impeachment proceedings against Donald Trump in 2020 and 2021, Turley charged that Biden and Hillary Clinton were co-ordinating an international censorship campaign in the U. S. and European Union, respectively:

> Biden's new Disinformation Governance Board is a telling replacement for the corporate censorship system. Now [Hillary] Clinton is looking to the Europeans to censor social media while Biden is turning to a type of Ministry of Truth.

Charges of the 'Orwellian' campaign to be led by 'Mary Poppins, the Speech Czarina' were ubiquitous, above all in far-right-wing media outlets. Yet some putatively non-partisan publications agreed. 'George Orwell call home', headlined *Bacon's Rebellion*, a non-partisan Virginia political publication with a libertarian bent. 'Comer, oversight Republicans blast Biden's Orwellian "Disinformation Governance Board"' headlined *Congressional Documents and Publications* on 29 April, reporting that James Comer (R-Ky) and other Republicans on the House committee on oversight and reform condemned the D. G. B. as a vehicle to suppress free speech.

True enough, the timing of the board's formation also raised eyebrows across the nation. Its 'Musky origins' possessed an Orwellian aroma that aroused olfactory attention even from those without the keen nostrils of Big Brother's father. That is to say, just days earlier, multi-billionaire Elon Musk – reportedly the richest man in the world, with a net worth between 250 and 300 billion dollars – had apparently bought Twitter for a mind-boggling $44 billion. He immediately gave notice that he would soon lift nearly all restrictions on 'free speech' that Twitter, following the lead of other Big Tech platforms such as Facebook, had instituted. In her first day on the job, Jankowicz expressed fear that Musk's free speech fetish would unleash a flood of disinformation. In an interview with National Public Radio (N. P. R.), she announced – without ever mentioning Musk by name – that she 'viewed with horror' the prospect of platforms run by 'free speech absolutists', given their willingness to circulate 'hate speech and hostile speech against marginalized citizens'. The board, she added, would certainly be reviewing closely the activities of all platforms and their content.

Even prominent Democrats voiced outrage that not only did Musk's intended purchase appear to be the trigger for the formation of the D. G. B., but the board also seemed to be the brainchild of Biden's predecessor, Barack Obama. According to Tulsi Gabbard, a 2020 Democratic presidential candidate and former Hawaii congresswoman, Obama was behind the effort to establish the D. G. B. 'Biden is just a front man,' Gabbard tweeted. She bemoaned that, just after Musk's announced plan to purchase Twitter in mid-April, 'Obama said that social media censors "don't go far enough" so the government needs to step in to do the job. Six days later, Homeland Security rolls out the "Ministry of Truth" (a.k.a Disinformation Governance Board).' She did not mince words about her fellow Democrats and the former 'Liar-in-Chief':

> The Democrats have zero credibility when it comes to censoring disinformation. They are the chief purveyors of disinformation. They are willing to lie without conscience to achieve their political objectives, and Obama has been the Liar in Chief.

JOHN RODDEN

Did Elon Musk's anticipated purchase of Twitter trigger the D. G. B.'s formation? Was the timing merely coincidence? Was Obama pulling the strings of his former vice president, now in the Oval Office?[1]

True enough, in a much-publicised speech at Stanford University on 21 April – just one week earlier – Obama specifically demanded that 'government take a larger role' in monitoring the release of information in the public sphere. The Biden administration evidently responded with the D. G. B. Given that platforms such as Facebook, Instagram and YouTube had readily cancelled subscribers or deplatformed them – and so, too, had Twitter – Obama's warning appeared directed at the policy change at Twitter that Musk was planning. And this would have included allowing Donald Trump, who had been banned from Twitter since January 2020 and the '6 January Insurrection', to receive back his account. Suddenly, therefore, under the wing of Musk – a vocal free speech advocate and a multi-billionaire – one of the Big Four in the world of Big Tech was 'opening up the floodgates of hate', as several left-wing supporters of the D. G. B. worried, echoing President Obama's speech.

DUCKSPEAKING ACROSS THE AISLE?

Within forty-eight hours of the founding of the D. G. B., with tens of thousands of references to its 'Orwellian' character and 'Big Brotherish' intent, the heavy hitters in the Republican Party weighed in. If the Disinformation Governance Board were, indeed, an embarrassing and ridiculous instance of Newspeak, as several liberal commentators acknowledged, evidence of what could be termed 'Newspeak Bipartisanship' was not in short supply. Or to borrow a coinage from another Orwell satire, *Animal Farm*, elephants and donkeys were happily quacking their talking points: 'duckspeaking' across the aisle.

On Friday, 29 April, potential Republican presidential candidate and Florida Governor Ron DeSantis took aim at the Biden administration's effort to have the Department of Homeland Security educate the public about disinformation, arguing that the D. G. B. was akin to Orwell's Ministry of Truth. DeSantis said the effort really amounted to a war against conservative dissent against a 'decaying and discredited ruling elite in this country'. 'You cannot have a Ministry of Truth in this country,' DeSantis said. 'We're not going to let Biden get away with this one. We will be fighting back.' DeSantis referred to the proposed board as a 'belated April Fool's joke' but one with a malign intent: to 'stifle dissent'.

Hours later, DeSantis was seconded by House Minority leader Kevin McCarthy: 'The same party that spent years promoting the Russia collusion hoax, suppressed the Hunter Biden laptop story & equated parents to terrorists believes it has credibility to control your speech,' McCarthy tweeted. 'Biden must immediately abandon his plan to create an Orwellian Ministry of Truth.'

That same day *Newsweek.com* reported that Rudy Giuliani, Trump's former lawyer, also lambasted the D. G. B. as a 'Ministry of Truth'. Giuliani, infamous for his blooper in 2019 that 'facts aren't facts', taunted Jankowicz as 'the whack-a-doodle Biden put in charge of the Ministry of Truth'.

Republican, conservative and libertarian journalists, tweeters and bloggers followed up with a steady barrage of attacks on the D. G. B. and Nina Jankowicz, who was morphing from Mary Poppins into the Wicked Witch of the West (Wing). 'Biden's Disinformation Governance Board = Orwell's *1984*,' headlined *The Oregon Catalyst*, a conservative online politics blog, suggesting that the D. G. B. (a.k.a. 'the speech police') would serve the Biden administration's political aims and branding anyone voicing statements critical of the Democrats' agenda a 'thought criminal'.

Surprised by the unexpected backlash to the formation of their disinformation unit within Homeland Security, its cabinet head, secretary Alejandro Mayorkas, and other administration officials took to the Sunday TV shows and signalled supporters to launch an online counter-offensive. On two Sunday morning TV interview shows, secretary Mayorkas reassured viewers that the D. G. B. would focus on online threats from abroad and would not monitor Americans citizens' Facebook, Twitter and other social media posts. Backpedalling in the face of stiff questioning, Mayorkas allowed that the initial explanations about the D. G. B.'s purview were regrettably imprecise, giving rise to misconceptions. He also uneasily admitted that, when he had originally hired her, he was 'not aware' that Jankowicz had discredited the Hunter Biden laptop story. Mayorkas reiterated that it was part of a concerted international push to counteract and restrict extreme, anti-government groups and foreign propaganda on Facebook, YouTube, Twitter, Instagram and other social media sites. The departing White House press secretary, Jen Psaki, also emphasised that the D. G. B.'s mission was 'protecting privacy, civil rights and civil liberties and the First Amendment' – even as critics responded acridly that a Mary Poppins taking aim at 'free speech absolutists' scarcely sounded like a champion of the First Amendment.

Only half-acknowledged by secretary Mayorkas and the Biden administration, however, was that the head of the D. G. B. herself repeatedly seemed to contradict them, urging that punitive measures be taken against U. S. citizens – for example, against men poisoned by 'toxic masculinity' who make women, 'especially non-white women', feel unsafe online, as she told N. P. R. As the *Wall Street Journal* noted, whereas Mayorkas repeatedly maintained that the D. G. B.'s jurisdiction would be limited to 'disinformation from Russia, from China, from Iran, from the cartels', Jankowicz happily defined its purview to extend to 'gendered and sexualized disinformation'.

Meanwhile, numerous liberals and leftists stepped up to support the D. G. B. and Jankowicz, charging that conservatives were spreading disinformation about the disinformation board. A *Washington Post* editorial headlined, 'Ignore the hysteria over the Disinformation Governance Board', because the D. G. B. would do a 'great deal of good'. The Poynter Institute quoted Jen Psaki that the D. G. B. 'will share best practices for countering disinformation purveyed by enemies of the U.S.'. (Critics noted that Poynter is funded by left-wing billionaire George Soros.) *Protocol* published an article that explicitly defended Jankowicz: 'Bad faith arguments abound, most of them focused on Jankowicz.' Horror writer Stephen King agreed, tweeting 'I stand with Nina Jankowicz' on Twitter.[2]

Speaking to *Insider*, Media Matters for America associate research director Kayla Gogarty accused D. G. B. critics of spreading 'conspiracy theories'. She added: 'Conservatives push bad-faith attacks under the guise of "free speech" in response to anything that they perceive will stymie their ability to push falsehoods and conspiracy theories.' The *Insider* story concluded: 'Right-wing politicians and pundits have misleadingly framed the [D. G. B.] group as a propaganda arm.'

MCCARTHYISM 2022 – THE RED AND THE BLUE

Undaunted and remaining sceptical, Republican critics proposed legislation to defund the D. G. B., which would render it nothing more than an empty shell. Touting his proposed legislative bill, S.4124, Senator Tom Cotton, of Arizona, declared that the D. G. B. was 'unconstitutional', 'un-American' and 'an idea popular with Orwellian governments everywhere'. Other conservatives simply called on the administration to disband the D. G. B. They were joined by 20 attorney generals from 18 red and two blue states across the U.S., all of whom objected to the 'McCarthyite speech policing' of the administration and reminded the president that 'the Ministry of Truth described in *1984* was intended as a warning against the dangers of socialism, not as a model government agency'. (Of course, Orwell intended neither, at least not in those terms.) Conservatives and libertarians also revived satirical anti-Obama chants of yore ('Yes, we scan!') that had gone viral when news broke in 2014 about Obama administration-approved government surveillance programs targeted at U. S. citizens under the auspices of the National Security Agency and F. B. I.

More and more Republican leaders joined the chorus. 'Rick Scott sounds warning about Homeland Security "thought police"' headlined the political blog *Florida Politics* on 3 May, referring to a speech by the state's senior senator. On 4 May, *Newsweek.com* ran a report headlined: 'GOP senator asks if Biden's "Ministry of Truth" will probe Lewinsky scandal', reporting that, during a hearing held by the Senate appropriations committee aimed at countering the spread of false information, Senator John Kennedy, of Louisiana, asked secretary Alejandro Mayorkas if his agency and the D. G. B. would investigate the 1990s scandal involving President Bill Clinton and former White House intern Monica Lewinsky. (Mayorkas replied that Homeland Security would investigate only 'threats to national security'.)

As the controversies about the D. G. B. continued through one news cycle after another, more observers sounded off. Pulitzer Prize-winning independent journalist Glenn Greenwald dismissed Jankowicz's alleged credentials as a 'disinformation specialist' in a *Substack* article on 4 May. Calling her 'a despotic imbecile – a cartoon figure spouting nonstop lies', he asked: 'But even if she weren't … what kind of person proudly [becomes] head of a Disinformation Governance Board?' Greenwald added:

> The concept of 'anti-disinformation expert' is itself completely fraudulent. This is not a real expertise but rather a concocted title bestowed on propagandists to make them appear more scholarly and apolitical than they are. There is no conceivable circumstance in which a domestic law enforcement agency like DHS should be claiming the power to decree truth and falsity. The purpose of Homeland Security agents is to propagandize and deceive, not enlighten and inform. The level of historical ignorance and stupidity required to believe that US Security State operatives are earnestly devoted to exposing and decreeing truth is off the charts. That nobody should want the US Government let alone Homeland Security arrogating unto itself the power to declare truth and falsity seems self-evident.

Nina Jankowicz herself did not lie low. Asked a week later on 12 May how the D. G. B. might handle Elon Musk's plans to open up Twitter, she suggested to a sympathetic Terry Gross on N. P. R.'s *Fresh Air* programme that D. G. B.-authorised Twitter users should 'add context' to tweets. She proposed that Twitter users who were 'verified' as 'legitimate' might place 'context' over tweets that needed it. 'Verified people can essentially start to edit Twitter,

JOHN RODDEN

the same sort of way that Wikipedia is, so they can add context to certain tweets.' Her example was a tweet by Donald Trump, still banned from the platform: 'Just as an easy example, not from any political standpoint, if President Trump were still on Twitter and tweeted a claim about voter fraud, someone could add context from one of the sixty lawsuits that went through the court or something that an election official in one of the states said.'

Elon Musk retorted later that day: 'Even though I think a less divisive candidate would be better in 2024, I still think Trump should be restored to Twitter.' He wanted no 'added context' determined by 'verified people'. Free speech advocates such as the Ukrainian-Jewish M. I. T. professor and podcaster Lex Fridman saluted Musk:

> Agreed. Permanent ban [of Trump] increased division, resentment, and hate in the world, not decreased it. It just moved it off the platform. Conversation is the only thing we have to heal the division and celebrate our common humanity.

Musk concurred. 'Exactly,' he tweeted. The American public seemed to agree. Some 59 per cent of U. S. voters expressed greater alarm about government-imposed limitations on free speech ('government choosing what's allowed') than 'disinformation and fake news', according to a Scott Rasmussen national survey also released that day, 12 May. Indeed, 48 per cent endorsed that statement that the D. G. B. 'will be used mainly to silence opposing viewpoints'.

By the second and third weeks of May, the D. G. B. debate had spread wings, crossed the Atlantic and was commanding headlines from mainstream news outlets abroad. Generally speaking, reports were scathing in their denunciation and mockery of Biden's 'speech police' and his Orwellian-sounding Disinformation Governance Board. *The Times*, of London, described Jankowicz on 9 May as 'a cross between Madame Mao and Bette Midler' and derided the Biden administration for 'blurring the line between genuine security threats and political or social differences' of opinion. 'Censorship,' *The Times* concluded, 'is never the right answer to disinformation.'

The conservative *Sunday Telegraph* concurred. 'Joe Biden's New Ministry of Truth puts the US on the fast track to an Orwellian nightmare,' declared Zoe Strimpel on 15 May. The D. G. B. was 'definitely foolish and possibly sinister' because it blatantly revealed 'the state meddling in areas it ought not to' – and it was 'chilling' that Biden officials didn't see that. Strimpel went on:

> The Orwellian name of the Democrats' new 'Disinformation Governance Board' need not have instantly repelled people like me. People who are truly worried by the barrage of harmful

rubbish [note that] those such as my taxi driver in Devon last week have been drinking up thirstily from the internet's many poisoned udders. Said taxi driver was an intelligent mother of two, living in the middle of nowhere, and disinformation, fake news and the conspiracy theories they stoke had got to her. She believed everything from the idea that wearing a mask is lethal for personal health, to that of the Ukraine war being cooked up by agents in a shadowy but preordained new world order, to the hypothesis that Elon Musk wants to implant scorpion-shaped devices inside all our brains.

Nonetheless, Strimpel regarded the D. G. B. as a nascent *Minitru* in the making:

Would it be nice to stamp out all those conspiracy theories, all that fake news? Of course. But regulation can quickly become censorship, and as some critics have noted, one woman's misinformation is another's information.

MARY POPPINS FLIES OFF

And then suddenly, just three days later, the winds changed direction. Faster than she could have sung the 'Let's Go Fly a Kite' chorus, Mary Poppins was gone – and the Jolly Holiday enjoyed by Beltway pundits over the haplessly named Disinformation Governance Board was over. The rise and precipitous fall of the widely dissed Disinformation Board caught everyone by surprise.

Unexpectedly, on 18 May, President Biden's new press secretary, Karine Jean-Pierre, announced that the D. G. B. was 'on pause' and that Nina Jankowicz was no longer at Homeland Security. Republicans expressed delight, though some conservative news outlets paused to wonder about the 'pause' announcement. 'If the Biden administration's picks such as Nina Jankowicz to head the D. G. B., or "Ministry of Truth" from George Orwell's *1984*, are any guide,' declared *Newsbusters*, 'the D. G. B. 2.0 will be no less authoritarian than D. G. B. 1.0, despite the departure of self-styled "Mary Poppins of disinformation".' Representatives of the conservative Washington-based Heritage Foundation noted that former U.S. deputy attorney general Jamie Gorelick and former Homeland Security secretary Michael Chertoff (who had long argued that the Hunter Biden laptop story was 'Russian-inspired') were Homeland Security's new advisors on combatting disinformation. Two dozen Democrat lawmakers also signed a letter to Facebook-owned WhatsApp in late May warning company executives to target 'disinformation' on the platform, specifically disinformation threatening to the 'Latino population' susceptible to claims that droves of 'illegal aliens' were crossing Amerika's southern border every month.

JOHN RODDEN

Even Mary Poppins was sighted as she touched down on N. P. R. again, insisting on 26 May – as the nation was convulsed by the mass shootings in Buffalo and in Uvalde, Texas – that her Disinformation Board may have helped prevent the mass shootings by sniffing out the disinformation that 'plays a role in radicalizing people to violence. ... Violent extremism is begotten by things people see on the internet'.

So the board has been 'paused' – not disbanded – and the same may be true for Mary Poppins herself, who may return with the next headwind. In any case, the campaign against disinformation is not about to go away. With the U. S. mid-term elections just around the corner this November, gales of disinformation involving claims and denials and counterclaims about the election 'Big Lie' should be expected to follow – and D. G. B. 2.0, whether authoritarian or benign, may soon be on the way.[3]

Benign? Dusted off with a new name and a clear mission statement focused on disinformation from abroad, yes, it's possible – and quite possibly valuable. Revelling in the tragi-comedy of the Biden administration's series of pratfalls, starting with the D. G. B.'s haplessly 'Orwellian-sounding' name and continuing inept roll-out and inadequate vetting of Jankowicz (and lack of co-ordination between her and her Homeland Security bosses), Republicans and conservatives generally gleefully japed and jeered at the fiasco, tending to elide the serious matters that it was putatively created to address. No prominent Republican or conservative commentator acknowledged that heightened efforts are needed to combat foreign disinformation (particularly from Russia and China). Or that some regulatory mechanisms on platforms – comparable to those governing the mass media – merit consideration. After all, the major platforms today mainly operate, quite ruthlessly, through bots and algorithms that generate the siloed echo chambers responsible for the political gridlock in which 'We the people' find ourselves – and which mire us in a vicious cycle of ceaseless volleys, swerving back and forth between staggeringly unbalanced, virtually one-sided vituperations against M. A. G. A. meatheads and Bidenland wokesters.

How and where to draw the lines between exposing disinformation and imposing censorship? Ah, that is a difficult question. Nonetheless, difficulty and imprecision should not be equated with impossibility and futility. Meanwhile, both U. S. legislators and the American citizenry may do well to ponder the words of Justice Louis Brandeis almost a century ago, voiced in his famous opinion in the landmark free speech case (Whitney v. California, 1927). Faced with heated disputes about the factual accuracy of public statements and impassioned calls for government censorship, Brandeis wrote:

> If there be time to expose through discussion the falsehood and fallacies ... the remedy to be applied is more speech, not enforced silence..

NOTES

[1] The purchase of Twitter by Musk has been attended by the drama of a legal battle when he first resolved to back out of the $44 billion purchase and then proceeded to go ahead. In October it was reported he was under investigation by United States federal authorities for his handling of the takeover bid

[2] The blowback was fierce – and funny. 'Scariest stuff you've ever written,' Matt Gaetz, Republican congressman from Florida, replied. '*The Stand with Nina Jankowicz*. I love remakes,' tweeted Matthew Kolken, the former elected director of the American Immigration Lawyers Association's board of governors – referring to King's 1978 post-apocalyptic novel *The Stand*. Journalist Glenn Greenwald dubbed Jankowicz and King as political bedfellows: 'Fiction peddlers stick together'

[3] Indeed, before the summer was out, with the D. G. B. still on 'pause', the White House launched 'the Disinformation Task Force' – presumably to make sure that any D. G. B. 2.0 of the future would be free of the sort of political malware that infected the Jankowicz-led D. G. B. Among those who will sit on the task force are top Biden administration officials such as defense secretary Lloyd Austin, secretary of state Anthony Blinken, and secretary of homeland security Alejandro Mayorkas himself. Meanwhile, the attorneys general of Missouri and Louisiana filed lawsuits charging that numerous government officials, including Nina J. Jankowicz, colluded with Big Tech companies to censor free speech under the pretext of combating purported 'misinformation, disinformation, and malinformation'. The lawsuits are still (in late September 2022) pending. On these developments, see Catherine Salgado, 'MO and LA state AGs subpoena Biden officials and Big Tech giants over alleged collusion,' *Newsbusters,* 27 July 2022

NOTE ON THE CONTRIBUTOR

John Rodden is the author, most recently, of *George Orwell: Life and Letters, Legend and Legacy* (Princeton, 2020) and of a forthcoming study, *George Orwell, Plagiarist?*

ARTICLE

Orwell's Rats

Why is George Orwell's work so infested with rats? His fiction, reportage, correspondence, diaries and essays record this obsession, often in the most visceral of language, which intensified as he aged. Darcy Moore suggests the foundations of this ever-omnipresent fear and loathing may have originated from an experience during his first year of life, in India.

The apotheosis of Orwell's rat obsession, in *Nineteen Eighty-Four*, his last novel, is one few readers ever forget. Deep inside the ironically named Ministry of Love, in Room 101 where political prisoners are tortured, Orwell's protagonist, Winston Smith, is confronted with 'the worst thing in the world':

> There was an outburst of squeals from the cage. It seemed to reach Winston from far away. The rats were fighting; they were trying to get at each other through the partition. He heard also a deep groan of despair. That, too, seemed to come from outside himself.
>
> O'Brien picked up the cage, and, as he did so, pressed something in it. There was a sharp click. Winston made a frantic effort to tear himself loose from the chair. It was hopeless; every part of him, even his head, was held immovably. O'Brien moved the cage nearer. It was less than a metre from Winston's face.
>
> 'I have pressed the first lever,' said O'Brien. 'You understand the construction of this cage. The mask will fit over your head, leaving no exit. When I press this other lever, the door of the cage will slide up. These starving brutes will shoot out of it like bullets. Have you ever seen a rat leap through the air? They will leap onto your face and bore straight into it. Sometimes they attack the eyes first. Sometimes they burrow through the cheeks and devour the tongue.'
>
> The cage was nearer; it was closing in. Winston heard a succession of shrill cries which appeared to be occurring in the air above his head. But he fought furiously against his panic. To think, to think, even with a split second left – to think was the only hope.

Suddenly the foul musty odour of the brutes struck his nostrils. There was a violent convulsion of nausea inside him, and he almost lost consciousness. Everything had gone black. For an instant he was insane, a screaming animal. Yet he came out of the blackness clutching an idea. There was one and only one way to save himself. He must interpose another human being, the body of another human being, between himself and the rats.

The circle of the mask was large enough now to shut out the vision of anything else. The wire door was a couple of handspans from his face. The rats knew what was coming now. One of them was leaping up and down, the other, an old scaly grandfather of the sewers, stood up, with his pink hands against the bars, and fiercely sniffed the air. Winston could see the whiskers and the yellow teeth. Again the black panic took hold of him. He was blind, helpless, mindless (Orwell 1997 [1949]: 298-299).

Even before publication in 1949, Orwell's vivid prose deeply affected those involved in the production of the novel. Orwell's typist, Miranda Wood, found it hard to get 'the rat torture scene' out of her mind even after the manuscript of *Nineteen Eighty-Four* was dispatched to the publisher, Secker & Warburg (Orwell 1998 [1949-1950]: 306). Fredric Warburg wrote a report on that manuscript noting that it was one of the 'most terrifying books' he had ever read and that Orwell had given 'full rein to his sadism and its attendant masochism, rising (or falling) to the limits of expression in the scene where Winston [is] threatened by hungry rats which will eat into his face…' (Orwell 1998 [1947-1948]: 479-481).

Many viewers of the controversial BBC television adaptation of the novel in 1954 (including politicians who mentioned the show in parliament) had the same horrified reaction as Wood and Warburg to the sadism and torture (Cartier 2022 [1954]; Ryan 2018: 22-38). Michael Radford, in his brilliant film adaptation, conveyed the truly awful horror of Winston's torture to a new generation (Radford 1984). The viewer experiences the sheer visceral terror of those 'old scaly' rats with their 'yellow teeth' poised to attack Winston's eyes or burrow through his cheeks to 'devour the tongue' as O'Brien torments the prisoner with his commentary (Orwell 1997 [1949]: 299).

Orwell's fascination with rats, evident for many years before the publication of this final novel, chart both his personal and vicarious, literary experiences.

DARCY MOORE   ORWELL'S RAT OBSESSION

> There are rats, rats,
>
> Rats as big as cats,
>
> In the quartermaster's store! (Orwell 1997 [1938]: 54).

D. J. Taylor has explored Orwell's 'rat obsession' more thoroughly than other biographers noting, in *On Nineteen Eighty-Four: A Biography*, that it is such a fixture of his printed work 'that he can often seem like a kind of literary pied piper dancing at the head of an unappeasable furry brood that winds on from one book to the next' (Taylor 2004 [2003]: 143-146, Taylor 2019: 16-17). In the dirty kitchens of *Down and Out in Paris and London*, his first published book, rats munch on ham at the breakfast table and Orwell's obsession with trapping rodents debuts (Orwell 1997 [1933]: 105; 114). In *Burmese Days*, there is the horror, 'among the jasmine' of the 'large rat-holes' which 'led down into the graves' (Orwell 1997 [1934]: 249). In *Keep the Aspidistra Flying*, Gordon Comstock (and this is very odd even by Orwell's standards) feels that his landlady views female visitors as 'plague-rats' (Orwell 1997 [1936]: 118). Visages he does not like are 'rat-faced' and Gordon's 'hatred' of advertising finds a familiar form, as he stares at a poster for Bovex:

> The idiotic grinning face, like the face of a self-satisfied rat, the slick black hair, the silly spectacles. Roland Butta, heir of the ages; victor of Waterloo, Roland Butta, Modern man as his masters want him to be. A docile little porker, sitting in the money-sty, drinking Bovex (ibid: 14).

In *The Road to Wigan Pier*, Orwell explains how he was 'half afraid of the working class' who seem 'alien and dangerous' but desperately wanted to 'get in touch with them' and as such has to brave common lodging houses, which felt 'like going down into some dreadful subterranean place – a sewer full of rats…' (Orwell 1997 [1937-1939]: 141).

It is hardly surprising that rats are omnipresent in *Homage to Catalonia*, Orwell's account of his experiences in the trenches during the Spanish Civil War. His disgust is visceral when waking up, in the chaff of a mule stable where the soldiers bedded down for the night, discovering it 'was full of breadcrusts, torn newspapers, bones, dead rats, and jagged milk tins' (Orwell 1997 [1938]: 14). Unsurprisingly, he later confesses, after an even more disgusting experience, that if there is one thing he hates 'more than another it is a rat running over me in the darkness' – but at least he manages to give 'one of them a good punch that sent him flying' (ibid: 59). Notably, an 'exasperated' Orwell takes a pot shot at a rat with his revolver causing his trench to be shelled (Taylor 2004 [2003]: 145). In *Coming Up For Air*, the rats are killed as they flee 'the threshing machine' (Orwell 1997 [1939]: 69-70). Sarah, a character in this novel, 'lived in a filthy little rat-hole of a place in the slummy street behind the brewery. The place swarmed with children like a kind of vermin' (ibid: 41). Very charitably though, rats are voted in as 'comrades' after the revolution in *Animal Farm* but, somewhat predictably, became 'troublesome that winter' and were thought 'to be in league with Snowball' (Orwell 1997 [1945]: 52).

It is instructive to examine the nooks and crannies of Orwell's lesser-known writing (letters, diaries, articles and drafts) to explore further this obsession. In his earliest written record about rats, a letter written to his friend Prosper Buddicom in 1921 while a teenager, Orwell explained his approach to killing rodents:

> My dear Prosper,
>
> Thanks for your letter. It was most awfully good your shooting the two snipe & the woodcock. You ought to get at least one of them stuffed, I think. I have bought one of those big cage-rat traps. This place is over-run with rats. It is rather good sport to catch a rat, & then let it out & shoot at it as it runs. If it gets away I think one ought to let it go & not chase it. If they are threshing the corn while you are there, I should advise you to go, – it is well worth it. The rats come out in dozens. It is also rather sport to go at night to a corn-stack with an acetylene bycicle (sic) lamp, & you can dazzle the rats that are running along the side & whack at them, – or shoot them with a rifle. I rather wish I had my rifle here, as there are no rabbits.
>
> Au revoir, please give my regards (or whatever it is,) to your aunt & uncle & everyone.
>
> Yours
>
> Eric (Orwell 1998 [1903-36]: 78-79).

In a draft of *Burmese Days*, possibly written as early as 1926, Orwell describes an enormously fat, half-naked man with a 'pockmarked face' whose lantern shines on 'a bedraggled dead rat lying on the doorstep' with 'the stench' growing 'stronger each minute' (ibid: 101).

Orwell's diaries are filled with pithy comments regarding rats that most people would not bother to record, although one entry, about a character he met in 1931, while hop-picking, is memorable:

> Before this he had been vermin-man to – , and he told me that the dirt and vermin in – 's kitchens, even [their headquarters], passed belief. When he worked at – 's branch in T – Street,

the rats were so numerous that it was not safe to go into the kitchens at night unarmed; you had to carry a revolver (ibid: 223).

In one diary entry, written just before the outbreak of the Second World War, Orwell notes the 'rat population of G. Britain estimated at 4-5 million (Orwell 1998 [1937-1939]: 368). We can see this research data being employed in *Nineteen Eighty-Four*:

'Rats!' murmured Winston. 'In this room.'

'They're all over the place,' said Julia indifferently as she lay down again. 'We've even got them in the kitchen at the hostel. Some parts of London are swarming with them. Did you know they attack children? Yes, they do. In some streets a woman daren't leave her baby alone for two minutes. It's the great huge brown ones that do it. And the nasty thing is that the brutes always – '

'Don't go on!' said Winston, with his eyes tightly shut (Orwell 1997 [1949]: 151).

While living at Barnhill, on the Isle of Jura, where he wrote *Nineteen Eighty-Four*, Orwell noted in his diary (12 June 1947):

Saw the buzzard carrying a rat or something about that size in its claws. The first time I have seen one of these birds with prey.

Five rats (2 young ones, 2 enormous) caught in the byre during about the last fortnight. These rats seem to let themselves be caught very easily. The traps are simply set in the runs, unbaited & almost unconcealed. Also no precautions taken about handling them. I hear that recently two children at Ardlussa were bitten by rats (in the face, as usual) (Orwell 1998 [1947-1948]: 156).

The following year, Orwell is concerned that rats are in the haystack again (ibid: 470). Another family member, his sister Avril, noted (she took over writing in Orwell's diary when he was in hospital and had the challenge of managing the property alone) her limited success poisoning rodents and finding an 'almost fossilised' one in the rubbish (ibid: 489-491). Always a close observer of nature, Orwell expressed surprise in a *Tribune* article that 'they bred so late in the year' (Orwell 1998 [1943-1944]: 176) and is justifiably impressed that 'a barn owl destroys between 1,000 and 2,000 rats and mice in a year' (Orwell 1998 [1947-1948]: 434).

Orwell is rarely anything less than a contradictory, paradoxical figure. In 1948, he replied from his bed in Hairmyres Hospital to a letter from Celia Kirwan with the most remarkable, surprisingly counter-intuitive rodent anecdote from his time in Paris, during the 1920s, one could conceivably imagine:

> How I wish I were with you in Paris, now that spring is there. Do you ever go to the Jardin des Plantes? I used to love it, though there was really nothing of interest except the rats, which at one time overran it & were so tame that they would almost eat out of your hand. In the end they got to be such a nuisance that they introduced cats & more or less wiped them out (ibid: 344).

Sadly, Orwell was allergic to an experimental tuberculosis drug that would have saved his life. Around the same time he wrote to Kirwan, Orwell explained to another friend, employing another striking image, his plight:

> I am a lot better, but I had a bad fortnight with the secondary effects of the streptomycin. I suppose with all these drugs it's rather a case of sinking the ship to get rid of the rats (ibid: 321-322).

He must have liked the turn of phrase, as he was still using it the following year in correspondence:

> If necessary I can have another go of streptomycin, which certainly seemed to improve me last time, but the secondary effects are so unpleasant that it's a bit like sinking the ship to drown the rats (Orwell 1998 [1949-1950]: 16).

WHY RATS?

> 'I don't like rats, that's all' (Orwell 1997 [1949]: 151).

Why was Orwell so obsessed with rats? What was the root cause (if any) of his revulsion and why did rodents occupy his thoughts and fuel his creative energy so vividly? Taylor suggests 'some of the roots of this fixation lay in literature' and lists Beatrix Potter, a poem by W. H. Davies and a short story by M. R. James as examples (Taylor 2004: 143-144). Orwell could not escape rats in comics either. In 'Boys' weeklies', his ground-breaking essay on popular culture, he describes memorable cover illustrations:

> On one a cowboy is clinging by his toes to the wing of an aeroplane in mid-air and shooting down another aeroplane with his revolver. On another a Chinese is swimming for his life down a sewer with a swarm of ravenous-looking rats swimming after him. On another an engineer is lighting a stick of dynamite while a steel robot feels for him with its claws. On another a man in airman's costume is fighting barehanded against a rat somewhat larger than a donkey (Orwell 1998 [1940-1941]: 68).

DARCY MOORE

Whatever the source of this distaste, and literature was of fundamental importance to Orwell's childhood, the record of his personal experience with rats is extensive and, as we have seen, rodents scurry through most of his standard published works.

Orwell is particularly obsessed with babies being menaced by rats. *Gulliver's Travels*, a book he esteemed highly, as we can see from his essay, 'Politics vs. literature: An examination of *Gulliver's Travels*', was read and re-read, from boyhood until the last years of his life:

> I read it first when I was eight – one day short of eight, to be exact, for I stole and furtively read the copy which was to be given me next day on my eighth birthday – and I have certainly not read it less than half a dozen times since. Its fascination seems inexhaustible. If I had to make a list of six books which were to be preserved when all others were destroyed, I would certainly put *Gulliver's Travels* among them. This raises the question: what is the relationship between agreement with a writer's opinions, and enjoyment of his work? (Orwell 1998 [1946]: 428).

Swift's satire has an episode that is particularly pertinent, as we will see, considering his own childhood experience:

> … I awaked and found myself alone in a vast Room, between two and three Hundred Foot wide, and above two Hundred high; lying in a Bed twenty Yards wide. My mistress was gone about her houshold Affairs, and had locked me in. The Bed was eight Yards from the Floor. Some natural Necessities required to get down: I durst not presume to call, and if I had, it would have been in vain with such a Voice as mine at so great a Distance from the Room where I lay, to the Kitchen where the Family kept. While I was under these Circumstances, two Rats crept up the Curtains, and ran smelling backwards and forwards on the Bed: One of them came up almost to my Face; whereupon I rose in a Fright, and drew out my Hanger to defend my self. These horrible Animals had the Boldness to attack me on both Sides, and one of them held his Fore-feet at my Collar; but I had the good Fortune to rip up his Belly before he could do me any Mischief. He fell down at my Feet; and the other seeing the Fate of his Comrade, made his Escape, but not without one good Wound on the Back, which I gave him as he fled, and made the Blood run trickling from him. After this Exploit I walked gently to and fro on the Bed, to recover my Breath and Loss of Spirits. These Creatures were of the Size of a large Mastiff, but infinitely more nimble and fierce; so that if I had taken off my Belt before I went to

sleep, I must have infallibly been torn to Pieces and devoured. I measured the Tail of the dead Rat, and found it to be two Yards long, wanting an Inch; but it went against my Stomach to drag the Carcass off the Bed, where it lay still bleeding; I observed it had yet some Life, but with a strong Slash cross the Neck, I thoroughly dispatched it.

Soon after, my Mistress came into the Room, who seeing me all bloody, ran and took me up in her Hand. I pointed to the dead *Rat*, smiling and making other Signs to shew I was not hurt; whereat she was extremely rejoyced, calling the Maid to take up the dead *Rat* with a Pair of Tongs, and throw it out of the Window. Then she set me on a Table, where I showed her my Hanger all bloody, and wiping it on the Lappet of my coat, returned it to the Scabbard (Swift 2022 [1726]: 132-133, emphasis in the original).

Orwell's parents met in India and married during 1897. Eric, their only son, was born in 1903 in Motihari, where Richard Blair, his father, was stationed. However, Orwell was not to stay long on the sub-continent; it was completely routine for the children of the officials working in the Indian Civil Service to return to be schooled in England, while the men remained at their posts. Ida Blair, his mother, fled India with her two children sometime in 1904 (Bowker 2004 [2003]: 10). A pressing public health issue and disturbing event in her home hastened this departure. The district was being ravaged by plague (ibid: 9).

ORWELL IN COT BITTEN BY RAT DURING PLAGUE

From 1896, India suffered two decades of high death rates from this disease and low monsoonal rains and the cooler temperatures in the north of Bihar, where Orwell's family were stationed, made the rapid spread inevitable (Klein 1988: 727). The family had been living in one of the three colonial bungalows, at the European edge of the town, known as 'Miscourt' (an amalgam of 'mess' and 'court') overlooking the fields when an incident that would horrify any parent occurred (Harding 2000). Orwell, sleeping in his cot, was bitten on the leg by a rat (Venables 2022). Understandably, this horrifying incident must have hastened his mother's departure with her children to England.

Prosper Buddicom enjoyed teasing Eric Blair about his fear of rats (ibid). Family diaries reveal youthful conflict and rivalry between Prosper and Eric (Buddicom 1917). Eventually, in way of explanation, Eric revealed a tiny scar was on his leg (Venables 2022). Prosper's sister, Jacintha Buddicom, was cynical that a rat had caused the injury when told this by the young Orwell and felt

ARTICLE

he was exaggerating (ibid). Her younger sister, Guinever, believed him (ibid).

This oral anecdote (discussed by both Guinever and Jacintha Buddicom multiple times with their cousin, Dione Venables) about the infant Orwell being bitten by a rat does make a great deal of sense considering Orwell's life-long obsession with killing rats and concerns about the vulnerability of babies:

> 'The rat,' said O'Brien, still addressing his invisible audience, 'although a rodent is carnivorous. You are aware of that. You will have heard of the things that happen in the poor quarters of this town. In some streets a woman dare not leave her baby alone in the house, even for five minutes. The rats are certain to attack it. Within quite a small time they will strip it to the bones. They also attack sick or dying people. They show astonishing intelligence in knowing when a human being is helpless' (Orwell 1997 [1949]: 298).

Generations of readers have asked the question: Did Orwell really shoot an elephant or witness a hanging in Burma? There has been considerable effort expended attempting to find autobiographical evidence that these two events happened and although neither has been definitively verified, it is generally accepted that the answer to both questions is – probably yes!

Did Orwell tell his childhood friends the *truth* about being bitten by a rat? Probably! But either way, it certainly seems to be a large piece of the puzzle as to why Orwell was so obsessively interested in rats!

- Special thanks to Dione Venables and Lady Jennifer Brown for their kindness and intellectual generosity in sharing the letters and diaries in their possession.

REFERENCES

Bowker, Gordon (2004 [2003]) *George Orwell*, London: Abacus

Buddicom, Lilian (Jacintha's aunt) (1917) Diary (unpublished)

Cartier, Rudolph (2022 [1954]) *Nineteen Eighty-Four* (Bluray), London: BFI

Crick, Bernard (1992 [1980]) *George Orwell: A Life*, Harmondsworth, Middlesex: Penguin, second edition

Davison, Peter (2013) *George Orwell: A Life in Letters*, New York: Liveright

Harding, Luke (2000) Shadows of Orwell, *Guardian*, 24 June. Available online at https://www.theguardian.com/books/2000/jun/24/georgeorwell.classics, accessed on 23 July 2022

Klein, Ira (1988) Plague, policy and popular unrest in British India, *Modern Asian Studies*, Vol. 22, No. 4 pp 723-755. Available online at http://www.jstor.org/stable/312523, accessed on 23 July 2022

Orwell, George (1997 [1933]) *Down and Out in Paris and London, The Complete Works of George Orwell – Vol. I*, Davison, Peter (ed.) London: Secker & Warburg

Orwell, George (1997 [1934]) *Burmese Days, The Complete Works of George Orwell – Vol. II*, Davison, Peter (ed.) London: Secker & Warburg

Orwell, George (1997 [1937]) *The Road to Wigan Pier, The Complete Works of George Orwell – Vol. V*, Davison, Peter (ed.) London: Secker & Warburg

Orwell, George (1997 [1938]) *Homage to Catalonia, The Complete Works of George Orwell – Vol. VI*, Davison, Peter (ed.) London: Secker & Warburg

Orwell, George (1997 [1945]) *Animal Farm, The Complete Works of George Orwell – Vol. VIII*, Davison, Peter (ed.) London: Secker & Warburg

Orwell, George (1997 [1949]) *Nineteen Eighty-Four, The Complete Works of George Orwell – Vol. IX*, Davison, Peter (ed.) London: Secker & Warburg

Orwell, George (1998 [1903-1936]) *A Kind of Compulsion: The Complete Works of George Orwell, Vol. X*, Davison, Peter (ed.) London: Secker & Warburg

Orwell, George (1998 [1937-1939]) *Facing Unpleasant Facts: The Complete Works of George Orwell – Vol. XI*, Davison, Peter (ed.) London: Secker & Warburg

Orwell, George (1998 [1940-1941]) *A Patriot After All: The Complete Works of George Orwell – Vol. XII*, Davison, Peter (ed.) London: Secker & Warburg

Orwell, George (1998 [1943-1944]) *I Have Tried to Tell the Truth: The Complete Works of George Orwell – Vol. XVI*, Davison, Peter (ed.) London: Secker & Warburg

Orwell, George (1998 [1946]) *Smothered Under Journalism: The Complete Works of George Orwell, Vol. XVIII*, Davison, Peter (ed.) London: Secker & Warburg

Orwell, George (1998 [1947-1948]) *It Is What I Think: The Complete Works of George Orwell – Vol. XIX*, Davison, Peter (ed.) London: Secker & Warburg

Orwell, George (1998 [1949-1950]) *Our Job Is to Make Life Worth Living: The Complete Works of George Orwell – Vol. XX*, Davison, Peter (ed.) London: Secker & Warburg

Radford, Michael (2015 [1984]) *1984* (Bluray), London: 20th Century Fox

Rogers, Leonard (1928) The yearly variations in plague in India in relation to climate: Forecasting epidemics, *Proceedings of the Royal Society of London. Series B, Containing Papers of a Biological Character*, Vol. 103, No. 721 pp 42-72. Available online at http://www.jstor.org/stable/81315, accessed on 23 July 2022

Ryan, David (2018) *George Orwell on Screen*, Jefferson: McFarland & Company Inc.

Swift, Jonathan (2022 [1726]) *Gulliver's Travels: The Cambridge Edition of the Works of Jonathan Swift*, Cambridge: Cambridge University Press

Taylor, D. J. (2004 [2003]) *Orwell – The Life*, London: Vintage

Taylor, D. J. (2019) *On Nineteen Eighty-Four: A Biography*, New York: Harry N. Abrams. Kindle Edition

Venables, Dione (2022) Interview, 9 July

NOTE ON THE CONTRIBUTOR

Darcy Moore is a deputy principal at a secondary school in New South Wales. He blogs at *darcymoore.net* and his Twitter handle is @Darcy1968. His Orwell Studies Library can be accessed at darcymoore.net/orwell-collection/.

BOOK REVIEWS

Orwell and Empire
Douglas Kerr
Oxford University Press, 2022, pp 240
ISBN: 9780192864093 (hbk)

> Once there was a British writer, an Englishman who was born in India. He was privately educated in England, did not go to university, returned to the East after leaving school, and lived and worked there for a handful of years. Empire, and the relation between those in authority and those under authority, became one of the principal themes of his writing, both in journalism and fiction (p. 152).

In his excellent new book, Douglas Kerr convincingly argues that empire was central to George Orwell's cultural identity and that colonial life shaped the writer he became. Kerr's ideas – first explored in his earlier, concise work on the writer, about the 'familiar pattern' of Orwell's 'journey to the East' for one born into 'a family of the military and imperial class' – have been developed considerably (Kerr 2003: 6). By allowing 'Orwell to speak for himself' of 'the East' and focusing on the oft-neglected historical/cultural context in which he wrote, Kerr offers new insights into an 'eastward-facing Orwell, poised between the Anglo-Indian Rudyard Kipling and the Indo-Anglian Mulk Raj Anand' (p. 17).

The introduction, a masterclass in synthesis and originality, employs irony and motifs from Orwell's work to bring the 'strong oriental subtext' that 'ran like the great seams of coal' through British life, into focus:

> The national beverage of the British, consumed in stately homes and in the shelters of the homeless, and celebrated in a characteristic essay by George Orwell called 'A nice cup of tea', is brewed from the leaves of a plant that cannot be cultivated in Europe, but grows on the hillsides of India and China. Tea was not the only quintessentially English thing, important to Orwell, that was not English at all. The aspidistra, that hardy and inelegant plant once so common in English middle-class homes that Orwell made it a comic symbol of respectability in *Keep the Aspidistra Flying*, is also a botanical immigrant from

the East. In English country gardens, oriental rhododendrons and camellias and peonies flourished under their assumed European names (p. 1).

Orwell, despite his enthusiasm for English cookery, beer, pubs, gardening and a nice cup of tea is shown to be 'a lifelong immigrant' of sorts, 'reporting on England, like Kipling, as on a foreign land' (p. 8).

Kerr's ideas are structured into thematic and largely freestanding chapters: Animals, Environment, *Burmese Days*, Class, Empire, Geography, Women, Race, Police, The Law, and Literature. He compellingly challenges conventional narratives and tropes throughout and does not baulk at discussing Orwell's limitations – especially on race, women and as a novelist. His commentary on Kipling and Orwell, the 'twinned heraldic animals, the lion and the unicorn of modern British literature', is particularly insightful (p. 152). Usually viewed through the prism of their differences as writers, Kerr's list of similarities the men share includes that they were both:

- Anglo-Indians and Asian by birth;
- patriots but highly critical of their government and the citizenry;
- public intellectuals interested in raising the political consciousness of the nation;
- enamoured with nature and the English countryside, loved (and anthropomorphised) animals;
- men of principle but pragmatic about change;
- impatient with orthodoxy, theory and hypocrisy (pp 152-153).

Kerr details the lifelong intellectual quarrel Orwell had with Kipling, whom he 'worshipped' at thirteen when at prep school, 'loathed' at seventeen while a sixth-former at Eton, 'enjoyed' at twenty serving as a police officer in Burma, 'despised' at twenty-five while living a bohemian existence in Paris and was to rather 'admire' again by 1936, as a struggling professional author with three published novels (p. 155). Kerr sees Orwell's ambivalence as evidence of paradoxical feelings towards both empire and his Anglo-Indian heritage. Considering the influence of Kipling on Orwell's work published in the period 1931-1936 – such as 'A hanging', 'Shooting an elephant' and especially *Burmese Days*, where the Englishmen, who lounge at the club, are clearly Kiplingesque characters 'stripped of their glamour and charm' – the struggle is evident (p. 154). *Burmese Days* is a powerful, although limited, indictment of empire but the protagonist, John Flory, an English timber merchant, certainly understands the 'commercial motives' that underpinned British imperialism in a way Kipling never did' (p. 68).

Edward Said's analysis of European imperialism, in his seminal book *Orientalism* (1978), explored 'the East' as an invention of the Western mind. Imaginative writers, such as Kipling, were the intellectual lifeblood of this invention. Kerr is surefooted explaining why the term 'orientalism' (in lowercase) is vexed terminology rightly associated 'with mastery, selection, and prejudice' and necessarily employed to foreground 'the powerful oriental dimension' in the work of Orwell who:

> … struggled all his life, and not with complete success, to exorcise the Orientalism (in Said's sense) which came with his Anglo-Indian patrimony. The argument is that this is absolutely formative to his intellectual and political development. Replacing Orwell in the Orient – and examining the Orient in Orwell – are central to the ambition of this book to rehistoricize him (p. 4).

Kerr works hard to achieve that, knowing that the Anglo-Indians have 'disappeared from view as completely as the Elizabethan apprentice boys or the London Huguenots' (p. 5). He explains that the Anglo-Indians 'carried a geography, and a history, different from people who took their bearings unquestioningly from the Greenwich meridian' (p. 6). As Orwell knew well, it was nearly impossible to escape from the class into which you were born.

Kerr is rightly unconvinced about theoretical claims that suggest Orwell is a 'post-colonial writer' pointing out that the great anti-imperialist does not seem to have developed friendships with indigenous people in Burma (which may be understandable as he

Mandalay, Burma, 1923, courtesy of the Orwell Archive

was an imperial policeman) nor in London during the war (p. 75). Orwell was always sceptical about the realpolitik of a successful Burmese democracy (p. 8). *Burmese Days* makes little attempt to explore the private life of the local people and is most notable for descriptive passages of the country's natural environment. Kerr notes that U Po Kyin, the villain of the novel, was the name of the only Indigenous face in the famous photograph taken at the Police Training School at Mandalay in 1923 (p. 125).

Orwell, the Anglo-Indian, had, indeed, internalised a geography different from those whose bearings were taken from the Greenwich meridian. Re-reading *Homage to Catalonia* (on completing Kerr's book), I noted that Orwell's memories of the war in Spain are represented through the geographical prism of the sub-continent. He arrives back in Barcelona on the train, after several months at the front, which reminds him of an experience more than a decade earlier:

> From Mandalay, in Upper Burma, you can travel by train to Maymyo, the principal hill station of the province, on the edge of the Shan plateau. It is rather a queer experience. You start off in the typical atmosphere of an eastern city – the scorching sunlight, the dusty palms, the smells of fish and spices and garlic, the squashy tropical fruits, the swarming dark-faced human beings – and because you are so used to it you carry this atmosphere intact, so to speak, in your railway carriage. Mentally you are still in Mandalay when the train stops at Maymyo, four thousand feet above sea level. But in stepping out of the carriage you step into a different hemisphere. Suddenly you are breathing cool sweet air that might be that of England, and all round you are green grass, bracken, fir trees, and hill-women with pink cheeks selling baskets of strawberries. Getting back to Barcelona, after three and a half months at the front, reminded me of this. There was the same abrupt and startling change of atmosphere (Orwell 1998 [1938]: 87).

Britain's empire was never far from Orwell's consciousness. His plan to return to India, to work on a newspaper in Lucknow just before the Second World War, never reached fruition. Two subsequent, 'wasted' years at the BBC as a talks assistant, then as the producer broadcasting propaganda into the sub-continent is explored (albeit briefly) in several chapters. Kerr's commentary on Mulk Raj Anand insightfully unpacks Orwell's complex relationship to the politics of empire during this time at the BBC:

> Anand was an anti-imperialist, a socialist, and an Indian nationalist. This was tricky for Orwell, who was highly

suspicious of nationalism. But he defended Anand from charges of being anti-British and unfriendly to Anglo-Indians in his writing. He was impatient with Anand's politics for the same reason that he disapproved of Congress agitation for Indian independence from Britain while the imperial Japanese army was storming through Asia. But as a literary figure, Orwell had no doubt about Anand's value and importance (p. 165).

Anand believed Anglo-Indians were often out of touch with their own countrymen, as well as the sub-continent (p. 6). Orwell was very surprised that independence came so quickly after the end of the war for the Indian and Burmese people and Kerr notes that Orwell, wrestling with his illness and *Nineteen Eighty-Four* on Jura, wrote nothing about it (p. 166). The recent discovery of letters, written to David Astor from Paris in 1945, do reveal Orwell's strong desire to return to Burma as a war correspondent to 'report the closing stages of the campaign and interview some of the political leaders' (Keeble 2022: 6). This fact, unknown to Kerr on publication, further strengthens his thesis about the centrality of the sub-continent to Orwell's cultural, professional and imaginative identity. Kerr concludes by mentioning that Orwell, returning to 'the Anglo-Indian world of his youth', was working on a new short story, 'A Smoking-Room Story', when he died (p. 167).

Scholarly and readable, Douglas Kerr's convincing new book is an essential one for those interested in Orwell, imperialism and the legacy of empire. It is also worth returning to his earlier book (2003) to see the development of Kerr's thinking about Orwell and 'the East'. Highly recommended.

REFERENCES

Keeble, Richard Lance (2022) Letters from Paris throw new insights on Orwell, *George Orwell Studies*, Vol. 6, No. 2 pp 3-7

Kerr, Douglas (2003) *George Orwell (Writers and Their Work)*, Tavistock, Devon: Northcote House Publishers Ltd

Orwell, George (1998 [1938]) *Homage to Catalonia, The Complete Works of George Orwell – Vol. VI*, London: Secker & Warburg

Darcy Moore

Complete Drama Reviews by George Orwell

Cole Davis (ed.)

Norwich: Volitor pp 135

ISBN: 9781916363274 (pbk)

Complete Book Reviews by George Orwell

Cole Davis (ed.)

Norwich: Volitor pp 902

ISBN: 9780349141992 (pbk); 9781408707999 (hbk)

Revenge is Sour: Lesser-Known Short Works by George Orwell

Cole Davis (ed.)

Norwich: Volitor pp 360

ISBN: 9781916363212 (pbk); 9781916363229 (hbk); 9781916363236 (ebk)

BOOK REVIEW

The lifting of the copyright restrictions on Orwell's writings in 2020, 70 years after his death, was inevitably going to lead to an explosion of re-publications. One of the first off the starting block was the rather strangely titled, 432-page *George Orwell: Visions of Dystopia (Gothic Fantasy)*, published by Flame Tree Collections in January 1921. With an Introduction by Richard Bradford and a Foreword by D. J. Taylor (so a couple of big names there), it drew together a somewhat haphazard selection: from *Homage to Catalonia*, *Animal Farm* and *Nineteen Eighty-Four* plus extensive extracts from *Down and Out in Paris and London* and *The Road to Wigan Pier* – along with brief extracts from Jack London's *The Iron Heel* and Yevgeny Zamyatin's *We*.

Also appearing last year were these three collections from Volitor. While their website (volitorbooks.com) publicises just these Orwell re-prints (though no purchasing details are provided), the company is clearly ambitious. They write: 'Literary fiction is an interest. Only potential Booker Prize winners should apply (no modernism please).' Cole Davis provides the Introductions: those for the first two being, unusually, adapted from presentations he has given at Yelets State University, Russia. But Davis is clearly not short of prominent contacts in the Labour Party: Lord Desai (in a Foreword), Charles Clarke, former home secretary, and Neil Kinnock, former leader (on the back cover), all have extremely positive words to say about *Revenge is Sour*.

Orwell's drama and film reviews (mainly for *Time and Tide*, the vaguely right of centre journal published by Margaret, Lady Rhondda) have not received the academic, critical attention they deserve. Perhaps the best analysis of the film reviews is by my late friend and University of Lincoln colleague, John Tulloch. His chapter 'Sceptic in the palace of dreams: Orwell as film reviewer' appears in *Orwell Today* (Abramis: 79-101), which I edited in 2012. All the 45 films Orwell reviewed are analysed with the details of the director, leading actors, date of publication, plus additional comments presented in tabulated form. Tulloch concludes:

> He shared in many of the standard prejudices of the Thirties intellectual against film – it was a mass art, machine-made by capitalism, producing low-grade rubbish for working class consumption. … Nevertheless, the reviews contain some valuable insights and embody a developing vision of the possibilities of film, both in its degraded form as a mass-produced mechanism for propaganda and escapism and an agency through which contrary, humane perceptions can be articulated. Orwell made heroic efforts to overcome his inbuilt class prejudices, and cultivated a belief in the innate human values of ordinary people and their capacity to remake society' (ibid: 98).

There is no such detail nor analysis here. Davis, rather, begins his Introduction examining the questions: 'Why was George Orwell important during the Cold War?' and 'Was his development down to luck?' According to Davis, one of the chance events was his decision to fight in the Spanish Civil War. 'His courage as a soldier had an underlying factor: he was rather reckless' (p. 2). Orwell's witnessing the betrayal of the revolution by the communists in Spain was another 'chance event' that was the 'beginning of Orwell's vendetta with extremism' (ibid). But Davis adds that there were many ways in which Orwell 'made his luck' (p. 3): 'Over the years, he had perfected his writing style, and he had tirelessly investigated social conditions. This made his commission to the north of England [to research the plight of the poor, the miners and the unemployed] more likely. It also meant that his last conventional novel, *Coming Up For Air*, sold well. An audience was prepared for *Animal Farm* and *Nineteen Eighty-Four*' (ibid).

Davis goes on to examine the reviews but rather too superficially. His drama reviews could have been placed in the context of his life-long love of the theatre, begun when he performed in a 'dramatic entertainment' 'Mr Jingle's wooing' (based on a Charles Dickens excerpt) at St Cyprian's prep school in 1916. While still a youth, Orwell composes a three-act play, 'The man and the maid' and Jacintha Buddicom, in her remarkable memoir of her times spent with the young Eric Blair (as he then was) on his school holidays, *Eric & Us* (2006 [1974]) tells of their voracious reading together – in particular, Shakespeare's plays and sonnets. Orwell writes another play, *King Charles II* (*CWGO* X: 294), for his pupils at The Hawthorns High School for boys, in Hayes, Middlesex, in 1932 – and it appears as *Charles I* which Dorothy Hare produces in his novel, *A Clergyman's Daughter* (1935). In chapter 3 of the novel, Dorothy spends a night with the down-and-outs in Trafalgar Square (Orwell clearly milking his experience as a tramp) and the whole episode appears in the form of a theatrical pastiche of the 'Nighttown' sequence of James Joyce's *Ulysses*.

It may also have been useful to highlight Orwell's wit and love of bawdy. Of Ariel, in a review of *The Tempest* at the Old Vic (p. 8), he says he 'was horribly whimsical and indulged in exaggeratedly homosexual mannerisms, a sort of Peter Pansy'. In Noel Coward's *I'll Leave it To You*, it's the humour that particularly appeals to him: 'It may be hard to believe that such nonsense can be charming, but it is so because of the easy dialogue which sometimes rises to the level of real funniness' (p. 22). While in his review of Vernon Sylvaine's farce, *Women Aren't Angels*, on 27 July 1940, he revels in the bawdy humour. The 'adultery-and underwear motif is pushed to the extreme limit of decency and sometimes a little beyond it, to the delight of the audience' with Robertson Hare, at one point, wearing a kilt 'incidentally solving the famous problem of whether they wear anything underneath' (p. 31).

Much of the rest of his theatre reviewing is dreary – and clearly Orwell was not getting much fun out of it. In his diary of 17 June 1940, he confides: 'Nowadays when I write a review, I sit down at the typewriter and type it straight out. Till recently, indeed till six months ago, I never did this and would have said that I could not do it. Virtually all that I wrote was written at least twice and my books as a whole three times – individual passages as many as five or ten times. It is not really that I have gained in facility, merely that I have ceased to care, so long as the work will pass inspection and bring in a little money. It is a deterioration directly due to the war' (*CWGO* XII: 187). But he comes to life in his review of Shakespeare's *King John*, on 19 July 1941, where he draws out some contemporary connections: 'The Papal legate, inciting France to attack England, is curiously reminiscent of the League of Nations. … There is a scene which would have delighted Marx in which everyone decides to obey or disobey the Pope according to his own economic interest. Even the Quisling motif is represented by the three English aristocrats who turn traitor when the French invade England, hurriedly changing sides again at the last moment' (p. 111-112).

Davis has done Orwellian scholars a great favour by drawing together all of his book reviews (I counted 530), though without any annotations, into one massive, 902-page tome. They are now crying out for serious, critical attention. Davis begins his Introduction with a useful, condensed, 10-page outline of Orwell's life and writing career. But again, the overview of the reviews is disappointing being descriptive rather than analytical.

In his celebrated essay, 'Confessions of a book reviewer' (Anderson 2006 [1946]: 314-316]), Orwell describes the job of reviewing books as a 'quite exceptionally thankless, irritating and exhausting job' (315). But he is ambivalent on most issues and in his 'Confessions' essay for the leftist journal, *Tribune*, where he is literary editor from 1943-1945, he is being ironic, deliberately self-effacing and humorous. Some of his most distinguished essays, in fact, focus on writers such as Charles Dickens, Rudyard Kipling, Jack London, Jonathan Swift, Shakespeare, Leo Tolstoy, P. G. Wodehouse and W. B. Yeats. And he uses book reviewing to serve a number of purposes: to celebrate his favourite writers or damn those he detests, to display his wit, explore ideas, expound on topics he knows about or extend his knowledge into new areas, to feed his voracious reading habit and to keep abreast generally of the intellectual currents of his day.

There are lots of questions I have regarding Orwell's book reviews. For instance, how many of them were of English/British authors, how many French/Spanish/German and so on? What percentage were women writers? For how many different publications did he pen reviews? What areas did he cover (politics, literary criticism, religion, novels, histories, biographies, autobiographies, poetry, essay collections, re-publications of major works, travel writing)? And what were his favourite fields? What were the prominent stylistic features of his reviews? What evidence is there that he skipped – a topic interestingly discussed by Somerset Maugham in the Introduction to *Ten Novels and Their Authors*, of 1954 – in his reading? Now, with this text in my hands, I can begin to find some answers.

Revenge is Sour (£14.12 on bookdepository.com) brings together what Davis calls 30 'lesser-known short works' by Orwell. They include 'Clink' (1932), 'Charles Dickens' (1939), 'Mark Twain: Licensed jester' (1943), 'In defence of P. G. Wodehouse' (1945), 'Notes on Nationalism' (1945), 'You and the atom bomb' (1945), 'The sporting spirit' (1945), 'Reflections on Gandhi' (1949), three examples of his 1944 'As I Please' columns for *Tribune* and a number of book reviews. In his Introduction, Davis explains the reasons behind his selection: namely, current relevance, comparative rarity (somewhat debatable in a number of instances), excellence and importance in highlighting Orwell's development as a writer. Thus he writes:

> The otherwise clunky 'Clink' shows the inexperienced writer engaged in action research in London's East End. Orwell's increasing political sophistication emerges, for example, as a reviewer of Hayek and of Burnham, as does his changed view on warfare and even to some extent of his ideological rivals. His final completed work, a review of Winston Churchill's *Their Finest Hour*, is unusually magnanimous. George's essential kindness was usually kept in private quarters (p. 10).

The annotating throughout is rather slender – but Orwell's writing always remains a treat.

Richard Lance Keeble,
University of Lincoln

BOOK REVIEW

Becoming George Orwell: Life and Letters, Legend and Legacy

John Rodden

Princeton University Press, Princeton, 2020, pp 384

ISBN 9780691182742 (hbk); 9780691228419 (pbk)

If you were to ask a professor of English literature 'which is the greatest novel of the Twentieth Century?', then depending on their interests and nationality, they may reply *Ulysses, Sons and Lovers, The Great Gatsby, To the Lighthouse, The Plague* or dozens of other titles. If you were to ask a slightly different question – 'Which is the most *important* novel of the Twentieth Century?' – *Nineteen Eighty-Four* may be in the top five. Narrow the question down further to 'Which is the most important *political* novel of that same period?' and *Nineteen Eighty-Four* would likely win by a country mile.

I'm guessing that most readers of *George Orwell Studies* would agree. I'd probably answer *Nineteen Eighty-Four* to every one of the above questions, but I'm biased. John Rodden, one of the world's foremost academic experts on Orwell, goes even further, arguing that Orwell 'is the most important writer since Shakespeare and the most influential writer who ever lived'. As he admits, it's a big claim, but he provides enough evidence to keep literature departments arguing for years.

What does he base this big claim upon? Rodden gives us several reasons. First, there's the curious sense you get when reading *Nineteen Eighty-Four*, as well as *Animal Farm* and Orwell's most celebrated essays, that you're reading a dictionary of famous quotations. 'Big Brother is watching you,' Rodden points out, 'is the most famous and frequently cited line in twentieth-century literature – and no runner up is even close' (p. 22). No other modern writer, he argues, has added more famous words and phrases to the English lexicon: 'Room 101', 'Newspeak', 'doublethink', '2+2=5', 'all animals are equal but …', 'the Cold War' and the list goes on. Even his name has given us 'Orwellian'. Rodden's statistics on the quotation of Orwell's most-known phrases and ideas make a compelling case.

Then there's his popular success. Admittedly, as a measure this isn't foolproof. I loved reading the Harry Potter stories to my children as much as any parent, but I wouldn't rank J. K. Rowling's stories as among the most *important* books of modern times. The most read certainly, and perhaps the most loved. But we're dealing here with serious fiction, and Rodden points out that Orwell is the highest seller of serious fiction in any language. All of his books, even the weaker ones, are still in print seventy-two years after his death. (Looking at my bookshelf next to me, I have at least three copies of *A Clergyman's Daughter*, including a recent reprint by Penguin, even though that novel is surely not his best.) And the most famous of his works continually reappear at the top of the best seller lists. My local bookshop owner tells me she sells at least ten Orwell books per week, even more when the academic year begins and those school reading lists are brought into the shop by busy-looking parents.

Importantly, there's Orwell's success in influencing the way we think. Rodden points out that Orwell has provided not only the language but also the dystopian vision through which we have interpreted succeeding political eras: the rise of fascism, total war, the Cold War, the surveillance era and the era of Trump (think of Winston, in his cubicle producing all that fake news). There's a fair chance, too, that the age of climate change will also be seen partly through his lens – it being a battle of ideas and a battle over logic. Readers can research this for themselves by turning to Fox News, then the *Guardian*.

As Rodden points out, Orwell also provides the model of the engaged writer that is imitated by virtually every public intellectual today: the scribbler in the firing line, unafraid to be the conscience of her own side, reaching out to a non-academic audience using plain, transparent prose, with a scrunched-up copy of 'Politics and the English language' in her breast pocket for easy reference and hopefully to stop a bullet. Orwell practically invented the genre of engaged journalism in *The Road to Wigan Pier* and *Homage to Catalonia*. I don't know how many journalist friends of mine have told me that on their first day on the job the editor hurled a copy of 'Politics and the English language' in their direction with the terse instruction: 'Come back tomorrow when you've read it!' (I'm guilty of giving my juniors the same compulsory advice.)

We may add to Rodden's list, Orwell's style. Think of how many writers you know get about in battered corduroys, a thick dark cotton shirt, woollen tie and brown sports jacket with elbow pads. Their shoes may also be unpolished and they're likely to drink real ale. If Albert Camus was the model of coolness, Orwell was the model of the angry young man, and some of those kitchen sink dramas of the 1950s and early 1960s owe direct inspiration to him. Fashion always comes back – that's my excuse and I'm sticking to it.

In short, Rodden says, Eric Blair has become more than the writer George Orwell. He is 'Orwell!', 'a world historical individual', whose ideas touch on the universal concerns of humanity. How did this happen (p. 22)?

Rodden suspects it's not just down to the great writing, but good timing too. *Animal Farm* and *Nineteen Eighty-Four* arrived just as the Cold War began and television started to take off. The former book was an instant hit in America, where it was lifted into the best seller lists by the Book of the Month Club (a bit like being endorsed by Oprah), and the latter was made into a highly controversial BBC television drama that in just one week in 1954 reached the then-unbelievable audience of 14 million, elevating him into the literary stratosphere (think of what the invention of streaming services has done for Sally Rooney's *Normal People* and imagine her as having a rather stronger political message).

And what accounts for Orwell's continuing popularity? Again, timing. Orwell's death aged just 46, meant he wasn't around long enough to take the shine off his own literary achievements by taking unpopular sides during the Cold War. Imagine if in his sixties Orwell had been in favour of America's anti-communist crusade in Vietnam or in his 80s a patriotic jingo over the Falklands War. (My feeling is that he would have been neither, but that's an argument for another time.) Sadly for Orwell, he never got to become an old curmudgeon, banging on about the good old days (despite his fondness for the countryside of his Edwardian youth). If he preferred 1913 to the Thirties and Forties, then the rise of totalitarianism and tens of millions of dead suggest that he may have had a point. As a result, both sides could (sometimes plausibly) read into him

BOOK REVIEW

their own beliefs and desires and adopt him as their patron saint. As several recent titles suggest, the political greens may one day elevate him to sainthood as well.

And then there's the sheer class of Orwell as a writer and human being. Yes, he had his weaknesses, including some that in the age of #MeToo may not stand up particularly brilliantly, but as Rodden writes, few match him for intellectual integrity, moral courage and literary excellence.

Imitating O'Brien in Room 101, Rodden could sum up Orwell's fame like this: intellectual integrity + moral courage + literary excellence x television = enduring greatness. Anyone who wants to understand what made George Orwell into 'Orwell!' is going to need John Rodden's new book, now out in paperback, on their shelves.

Dennis Glover

- Dennis Glover is the author of the novel *The Last Man in Europe* (Black Inc. 2017) which dramatizes Orwell's struggle to write *Nineteen Eighty-Four*.

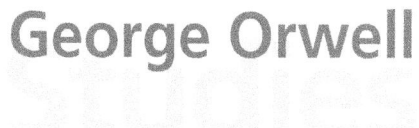
George Orwell

Subscription information
Each volume contains two issues, published half-yearly.

Annual Subscription (including postage)

Personal Subscription

UK	£39
Europe	£43
RoW	£45

Institutional Subscription

UK	£100
Europe	£115
RoW	£120

Single Issue copies can be purchased (subject to availability)

Enquiries regarding subscriptions and orders should be sent to:

>Journals Fulfilment Department
>Abramis Academic
>ASK House
>Northgate Avenue
>Bury St Edmunds
>Suffolk, IP32 6BB
>UK

Tel: +44(0)1284 717884
Email: info@abramis.co.uk

www.ingramcontent.com/pod-product-compliance
Lightning Source LLC
Chambersburg PA
CBHW080438230426
43662CB00015B/2306